A PROMISE OF TOMORROWS

Bernadette M Redmond

1

'We are the children of our landscape; it dictates behaviour and even thought in the measure to which we are responsive to it'.

Lawrence Durrell; Alexandra Quartet

'Only an eejit goes out to slane the turf when the clouds are against the wind'

Words of wisdom by Uncle Martin Qualter, farmer and weather forecaster

Table of contents

3

Chapter 1

Wildlife in SE21.

Two pair of eyes stared unblinkingly at me seated on one of the back side seats of a battered twelve seater yellow Bedford van. They knelt facing me on the middle seat to scrutinize me in comfort. My month-old daughter slept in her bassinette beside me while on the opposite seat a carrycot held an eight-month baby, arms above his head and dead to the world apart from the occasional gentle sucking movements he made with his mouth.

'Sit down' the driver said firmly to the kneeling children, who totally ignored her.

'I only brought three of them in case you changed your mind if you met them en masse' she said cheerfully looking back at me through the van mirror.

My new employer, Ann, was a well built, bohemian looking woman, with hair twisted into an untidy bun, a face free of any trace of makeup and full of character rather than beauty. A doctor, with five children under ten, she handled the cumbersome van expertly and without apparent effort on our journey from Harrow-on-the-Hill to West Dulwich.

I had previously been to the Dulwich house to be interviewed so knew what to expect. On that occasion the three older children had been in Sussex with their grandmother and the younger ones sleeping. Shabby and untidy the house had seemed quiet and peaceful. My daughter and I would be expected to live en famille with me employed as 'mothers help'.

My room on the second floor was spacious and warm and overlooked the road and obliquely, Dulwich College Prep School. I would share this landing with Jane age four and, John, the baby who was currently sleeping in the dressing room adjacent to his parent's bedroom, would join us as soon as I had settled in. There was bathroom across the landing, a single bedroom converted into a kitchen and two double bedrooms, one accommodating Jane.

Peter, father of the children, had been inveigled out of his study near the end of the interview to give me the once over. A thin dark haired man in a leg iron, and also a doctor, he scrutinized me as thoroughly as his children were now doing.

'Your application makes you sound as if you can do everything apart from walk on water' he said humorously.

'Well, given time I'll probably master that too' I responded smartly much to his amusement.

His easy charm and droll sense of humour immediately put me at ease but disconcerted Ann because he began regaling me with horror stories about previous employees who had fled unable to cope with their children's unruly behaviour, and the lack of routine and consistency in the household.

A small grimy hand held out a match box towards me and said invitingly 'Would you like to see inside?'

I saw the glint of devilment in the eyes of the grubby handed blonde eight-year-old and remembered my Cousin Tommy Duggan's frog collection. 'Ok, let's have a look' I said encouragingly.

With his thumb, he gently pushed the matchbox open while holding it out in my direction. Much to his disappointment the ensuing screams were not from me but from the four-year-old Jane who took a flying leap into one of the front passenger seats of the van causing her mother to veer wildly across the road and yell impotently at her. Mid Sunday afternoon the traffic was sparse which probably saved our lives because seat belts were non-mandatory in 1960.

'Wow, he's a monster' I said nonchalantly reaching over and touching the pincer of an enormous shiny stag beetle which filled the box.

'Isn't he a bit uncomfortable in there' I asked without engaging my brain.

'Probably' said the budding entomologist as he tipped him out on my hand.

I knew this was a make or break moment and watched the look of glee turn to disappointment as I failed to react.

'It would be kinder to let him go' I told the little provoker as I offered the beetle back to him

Thus, was my first encounter with Mark's wild life enthusiasm. It was to be the first of many.

Chapter 2

Chaos and Mayhem.

The van crunched on the gravel of the crescent shaped drive in front of a big rambling detached house which so far I had only seen in the dark. In that era, Alleyn Park Road was a wide tree lined road of turn of the century large basemented family houses set back from the pavement by drives, and with generous back gardens. The freeholds were held by Dulwich College Estate a charitable foundation known formally as Alleyn's College of God's Gift making those leasehold properties and so affordable by impoverished professionals. Mark and Jane scrambled from the van and disappeared around the side of the house leaving Ann and I to manage both babies and my worldly goods packed in two suitcases.

The front door opened and a boy with a mop of brown hair came bounding towards us.

'Peter said to come and help' he explained smiling and extending his hand.

I had assumed this charmer was nine-year-old Simon but was thrown by his referral to 'Peter'.

'They all call their father 'Peter' Ann explained.

I had expected Simon to choose a suitcase to carry instead he took hold of the handles of the bassinette containing my sleeping baby. He was surprisingly gentle and careful so I curbed my urge to stop him letting him get on with transporting her into the house.

With everything packed away and Vanessa fed I answered Ann's call to come down to tea. Everybody was sitting at a large oil cloth covered farmhouse table in the dining area off a big kitchen. John, now awake was sitting in his high chair waiting to be fed. A big blonde baby he was the picture of placid happiness and good humour.

'This is Vanessa' I said introducing my daughter who was in my arms. She was small and neat with a head full of black hair and was still learning to focus on her surroundings.

'She looks like a doll' Mark said poking her to get her attention. I waited for Jane to join in since she had not said a word the whole journey. As I took a seat I realized we were a child short and learned that six-year-old Emma was in Sussex.

Tea, was a meal like Irish tea; something cooked accompanied by bread and butter, biscuits or cake. Lunch was the main meal of the day for the children, as was school dinner on school days. While Ann scooped a bowl full of yellow glop into John's willing mouth she explained that she would cook evening meals, ergo, dinner, for her and Peter and I would be responsible for family breakfast, lunch and tea.

I tried to keep my eyes averted from the appalling table manners of the three children.

'Like pigs at a trough?' Peter opined in a questioning tone as if expecting me to agree.

A memory of Theresa Donovan, my mentor when I started nursing rose to the surface. She had been referring to a table full of student nurses I has been looking at in horror as they gobbled their food in their allotted meal time.

'Our last help left because she couldn't bear to sit at the same table with them' he said watching me slyly.

'Well she obviously never ate in a hospital dining room' I responded tartly passing a slice of cake to Jane to discourage her from crawling across the table to reach it.

His face cracked into a wide smile, and with a nod and an excuse me, and an implied 'You'll do' he lurched back to the peace and quiet of his study. Engaged in this exchange I missed the cue that an altercation was about to break out between Simon and Mark so that Simon's smirk and Marks belligerent red face were already evident as the tussle at the table began. Ann was by then in the kitchen hanging washed clothes on a Dutch airer and seemed totally oblivious to the mayhem that had erupted at the table as they tried to stab each other with forks. I knew that by now they were beyond reason so putting Vanessa in her bassinette I grabbed a surprised Simon by the scruff of the neck, anticipating that Mark would follow and headed for the garden door.

Wrenching the forks from them I chucked both of them out with the explanation that I drew the line at cleaning up blood so if they were intent on killing each other to find some other way of doing so in the garden. Ann and I spent the next half hour in the kitchen which overlooked the garden clearing piles of unwashed pots and dishes and sorted out another wash for the launderette size Bendix while Jane played happily with John and I kept an eye on a sleeping Vanessa and the fighting brothers.

'How long will that go on for' I asked indicating the latter.

'It won't end until one of us intervenes' she said with resignation. 'Mark will never give up and Simon will never concede'.

'Let me give you a tour of the house before we separate them' she offered.

   Clockwise in the front hall the book lined room to the left of the front door was the sitting room. A portion of it, overlooking the front drive was partitioned off by a double-sided book case to form Ann's office. Next to it facing the back garden was Peter's study. He also had his book lined wall but apart from a few Virginia Woolf and Thurber books it contained little that was non-medical. Inside the back door was a cloak room, then two steps down was the door to the basement, and beside it the door to the dining room which was the length of the house, the dining area facing the front garden the kitchen end overlooking the back. Completing the clockwise orientation back in the hall was a wide staircase with tempting mahogany banisters and the door to by far the biggest room was the room that formed the front bay to the house. This was the playroom. Lino covered for ease of cleaning it was a huge nursery type room the centrepiece being a well-used rocking horse that had already lost his mane and hair. Adorning the wall facing the window was a large school atlas of the world still proclaiming its Empire status if a pink Ireland was anything to go by. Its uncurtained windows, in time, led to women ringing the front door bell to enquire, hopefully, if I was running a nursery

As we went up the stairs to the first floor she told me 'The children are not allowed in Peter's study and are not to go into the sitting room unless I am there' and as an addendum 'I don't like to be disturbed while I am working so I like them to knock'. Hmm

Four bedrooms, a dressing room and a bathroom on the first floor later she said 'You go and settle in and I'll see you in the morning'.

Said in a tone of voice that implied that she wished that I wouldn't, but I picked up the bassinet with a now irate baby wanting a feed and made for my room.

'There's no need for an early start tomorrow, it's half term' she added in a heart sinking rider.

Later, as I prepared for bed I saw something slithering from under my pillow. I knew it was unlikely to be poisonous so pursued it. It was a fully grown slow worm not unlike a baby snake to the uninitiated. 'Well Marky Boy, you'll have to try harder' I thought. Now if he had only presented me with a cockroach he would have had all the reaction he craved.

Chapter 3

Lily and Molly.

Apart from Vanessa waking twice to be breast fed I had slept well. I woke to a gloomy late February day. A pair of wide awake brown eyes gazed into mine. 'I'm hungry' said the formerly silent one standing by my bed. I looked at the clock and groaned. At a few minutes past seven the house was still quiet so I crept downstairs to get her a bowl of cornflakes which she consumed and took herself back to bed. I remember little of the next two hours apart from considering packing my bags and heading for Ireland to accept family offers to rear Vanessa while I completed my nurse training. Having already sat, and passed, the Hospital Finals at St. Andrew's Hospital in East London I only three months to go to achieve State Registration. It was a tempting proposition. When I had chosen to train at an East London hospital I had done so because I was impressed by the then matron, Grace Laing. She may well have been disappointed by my unplanned pregnancy, but she had done everything possible to ensure a smooth return to resume my training. This included sending me the course material being pursued by my Set.

However, it was the appearance of Lily Somers and Molly Wallace at 9.00am that swayed the balance. Lily, buxom, scarlet bow lipped, peroxide blonde hair curled under and netted like a WW2 munitions worker and a wraparound apron was our daily cleaner and, until now, occasional baby sitter. Cheerful and incapable of cleaning and talking at the same time I learned to keep any chat with her to her 10.30 coffee break. Her high pitched screechy singing as she worked took some getting used to and to this day I only have to switch on a Hoover to be haunted by 'Vilja O Vilja' from Franz Lehár's Merry Widow as Lily vied for supremacy. She had been with the family since they had lived in Brixton so had seen them through the worst eighteen months of their lives when Peter succumbed to the ravages of polio. She was therefore a great source of family lore.

Lily did 'the rough' as she told me. She was responsible for the bedrooms, the landings, the staircase, the hall, two bathrooms and the cloakroom and playroom. She considered the dining room and kitchen to be my domain. She has a rota for changing the children's sheets and towels which only affected me in the sense that I had to wash and dry them for Molly to iron. I had wondered why there were three Dutch airers in the house as well as a patio clothes line but I realized that with at least three loads of washing daily they would be well used. Lily fought a losing battle with Simon's untidiness and Marks wild life collection and confessed that she got no support from Ann.

'Mrs, D doesn't want to hear about problems' she reasoned astutely.

'Deal with the kids, then, if you have to, tell her, but don't expect them to quake in their shoes. They know that she'll have a rant but will never fulfil her threats'. Hmm

Molly, with the family for three years was scrawny with tight permed pepper and salt hair and had a hint of faded glamour exemplified by a refined use of a cigarette holder when she lit up. She wore a parlour maid type apron around her waist to indicate that she did no rough work. Molly came three mornings a week. Mondays and Fridays, she was responsible for cleaning Peters study, the sitting room cum Ann's office and their bedroom. She also oversaw the dispatch of the laundry box containing Peter's shirts and Ann's dry cleaning items on Mondays and checked and hung up the returned items on Fridays. Wednesdays, she did the ironing. Towels were put through the roller iron. Sheets were spray starched and followed and would have graced the beds of a 5* hotel. School uniform items were then pressed with the steam iron, but a constant bone of contention between her and Ann were items like socks, tea towels and underpants. Ann considered ironing them a waste of time.

'Mrs D, you're a professional lady, how can you let your children be seen dressed like gypsies' she would say disapprovingly?

'Suppose they had to go to hospital'?

To keep the peace, I used to crumple up knickers and socks to hide the evidence of a smoothing with the iron. I never understood the point of the argument since Molly not only completed the ironing within her allotted time but made time to tell our fortunes by regularly reading our tea leaves. Peter was always interested in this activity having perfected the arts of Palmistry and Phrenology as a medical student to earn money. When he read my hand, he told me I had a short life line, which I felt might well come true if I stayed in this household. Probably the reason why I never made a start on Proust!

Clarifying Lily's and Molly's roles I realized that mine was far from clear. Apart from having Sundays off Ann had been remarkably airy fairy about my hours and duties.

'Let's see what works' she had said reasonably having worked out my wages at £3.50 a week. Some weeks later, when I calculated my working hours that amounted to less than 6d an hour, a pittance in comparison to Lily and Molly!

Chapter 4

Battles and compromises.

That first week choosing when and where to make a stand with the children was easy. While it was possible to selectively ignore some behaviour, I decided that come yells and high water eating habits were going to be improved even if I had to starve them into submission. Underlying the problem was the fact that all children in the household old enough to reach a kitchen cupboard foraged for food. Constant grazing meant they were never hungry so they never wanted anything that resembled meat, or orange and green coloured veg, and would quite happily exist on cereals, biscuits and cakes, supplemented by fish fingers, spaghetti hoops and baked beans, the latter two eaten cold and straight from the tin. Ann willingly handed over the weekly provisions order to me, so I crossed off eight choices of cereal, selections of crisps, biscuits, cakes and ice cream and in came cheese, fruit, vegetables and yogurt. I reorganised the larder moving tempting items from the kitchen cupboards under lock and key until some progress had been made. The outrage on day one of the battle was ear shattering. I had set the table with a jug of orange juice and one of milk. The jugs alone were a foreign concept to these children as was the plate of pre-cut bread. 'You can have cornflakes or boiled egg and toast' I said firmly as I fed John cornflakes squashed in warm milk. Simon ignored me and went into the kitchen to help himself. The rearranged cupboards floored him and his rage was spectacular. He saw Mark grinning in amusement and made a lunge for him. 'Not until after breakfast' I said, placing myself in his way. He went off banging and screaming while out of the corner of my eye I saw Mark settling down to cornflakes. I made him toast, a treat they weren't usually allowed because they had at one time or another all tried to electrocute themselves poking knives into now defunct toasters. The last toaster had not been replaced so toast had to be made laboriously under the cooker grill. Jane eventually opted for an egg and soldiers having been completely thrown by having to make a decision at all. Each meal followed the same rule, a choice of protein and vegetables with puddings or fruit and homemade cakes to sweeten the routine. In less than a week a reasonable diet was being consumed by all. All helpings were pre-plated in good working class fashion to prevent inequality, reaching over people and to reduce mess. Even tho' knives, forks and side plates increased the washing up their presence transformed their manners.

It was Easter before I learned that they had always been capable of displaying good manners at their grandparent's home in Sussex and that it was only in their own home they behaved like chimpanzees. This is not surprising since there was no parental involvement at meals apart from Sunday lunch. Also, they got very little praise or recognition when they *were* well behaved, and little or no one- to-one time with either parent. What scant individual attention they got was usually precipitated by bad behaviour. An example of this lack of individualism was demonstrated by Ann's attitude to upcoming birthdays. She mentioned that she, Jane and Simon, had birthdays looming and that we should choose a day for a joint celebration. I had lived in a frugal household throughout my childhood but thanks to my thrifty grandmother I had always had a birthday celebration despite the fact Christmas was on the horizon. I don't think money was the issue here it was more a question of time commitment, but every child should have a birthday celebration and as far as I was concerned they would. Perhaps when there was a bit more structure, order and calm in the children's lives more family time would follow? As my Gran, would say 'If wishes were horses then beggars would ride'.

The cupboards were soon restocked without morsels of desire; however, Simon was still tempted to a bit of furtive foraging. Having spent an afternoon and evening feeling unwell the reason was found in his waste paper basket the following morning by Lily. He had consumed a large tin of Carnation condensed milk. Lily and I never mentioned it but at tea time I made it known that the fudge I had intended making as a special treat for Emma's home coming would not being materialising because the tin of condensed milk had disappeared. Puzzlement from two, slight tinge of pink from the guilty one.

Emma, a Valentine's Day baby, returned from Sussex to new rules and found me on good terms with her siblings which caused some tension. She was a bit of a pampered princess spending most weekends, half terms and holidays with her grandmother and Ann's spinster sister, Barbara. The latter lavished a lot of attention on her, treating her as a proxy daughter by ensuring she has a pony, membership of the local Pony Club, training to ensure she excelled at local Gymkhanas and an entrée into the local Hunt and County Set. Although only six this special attention made her an uneasy fit within the family, too bossy and self-opinionated for Simon to tolerate, in too much physical competition with Mark for his comfort and a bully towards the much quieter self-effacing Jane. The only one of her four siblings pleased to see her was John who shook his arms in the air with excitement. After a first petulant look on introduction she ignored me for the duration of tea. Eventually, glowering at me she asked

'How long are you staying'?

'Until the twelfth of never, or until hell freezes over, or until my luck comes up on Ernie, whichever comes first' I responded teasingly holding her hostile glare.

Simon and Marks hoots of laughter had her flouncing from the room. It was obvious that Emma did not appreciate persiflage.

'Can we have chips tomorrow' Simon asked noting I was in a good mood?

'Only if you pick your clothes up off the floor and hang them up for Lily' I said.

'What does *he* have to do' he said glaring at Mark.

'*He* has to have a bath, shampoo his hair and wash with soap' I said, expecting resistance.

I had learned that Marks reluctance to wash his skin was becoming a problem, the school having reported his refusal to shower after games. 'I like the feel of my skin when I don't wash it' he told me seriously. I had tried not to laugh having imagined all kinds of bullying problems and pissing competitions in the school communal changing room. I had elicited a reluctant agreement from him that skin must be cleaned once a week so this seemed like a good opportunity. They knew that making chips was a major hassle because we did not possess a chip pan and West Dulwich was too posh for a fish and chip shop. A chip pan had joined my list of 'must haves', but top of the list was a twin pram.

Chapter 5

Missing believed kidnapped.

Having been brought up in Dublin by a granny who was a connoisseur of bargain hunting and whose thrift and frugality had been a constant source of embarrassment to an ungrateful child, it did not take me long to realise that I was part of a household where money was tight. Furniture had been acquired through the beneficence of dead relatives or at auction sales were sellers were getting rid of outsize items to re furnish the sleeker houses of the beau mode. The two reliable sources of money that formed the budget were the family trust fund that paid the children's school fees and related expenses, and Peter's hospital salary as a registrar which kept a roof over our heads. Ann had more or less given up practicing medicine to pursue a career as an author and journalist, so her earnings were erratic and influenced what was left in the kitty at the end of the month. She supplemented her income by working as a locum NHS Clinical Medical Officer at Child Health Clinics on a sessional basis. My Gran would have found Ann's ideas on budgeting derisory though she would have admired her for doing so. From day one it was obvious that if I was to get out of the house with two babies I needed a double pram. A new one was out of the question so while Lily and Molly scoured the For Sale or Rent cards in their local newsagents I perused the small ads in the local paper.

A Rolls Royce of a pram was found with an asking price of 30 shillings. Since I had already reduced the provisions bill by nearly £5 a week I foresaw no difficulty in Ann funding it. A walk around to Rosendale Road nearby convinced her it was just what we needed so she pushed the empty pram home and John and Vanessa were ready to travel in style. It was an enormous twin hooded Silver Cross model in excellent condition and coped well with the demands put on it for the next four years.

Its very commodiousness meant that it accommodated two and eventually three babies and a dog and, as an added bonus, a substantial amount of shopping bags. I now had the freedom to get to the local shops and to cease being solely dependent on Buckley's deliveries. I discovered a small butcher's shop which, unlike Buckley's high class grocery emporium, sold offal and having been raised on offal, or 'awful', as we called it (sorry Gran!) I knew I could make nourishing meals for a fraction of the cost of the prime cuts of meat Buckley's boy was delivering. Likewise, there was a fruit and vegetable shop where I could pick and choose what I wanted knowing it had come straight from Covent Garden market. However, the local Mecca of markets was at that time a bus ride away in Brixton, the family's former neighbourhood. Its multicultural stalls and exotic food had to wait several years for our renewed custom.

Ann, seeing the advantages of an ample pram began taking John and Vanessa along to the shops when she had an article or commissioned review to post. She would then do a bit of shopping and wheel the sleeping baby's home leaving them under the tree in the front garden. I would let them sleep until one or the other showed signs of restlessness. I checked on them by keeping them under observation from the dining room window. On this occasion the pram wasn't visible so I assumed Ann had left it in the shelter of the garage around the side of the house. I opened the backdoor but could see no sign of sleeping babies or pram. Despite the fact that there was half an acre of garden, the distant third being jungle, it is difficult to hide a tank of a pram. In a heart stopping moment my stomach turned over as I realised that John and my daughter had been abducted. I ran to the sitting room bursting in without notice stammering out disjointed sentences containing the words 999, police, and kidnap. Ann sat riveted with terror, then with dawning horror.

'Oh, God Almighty' she said through voice cords struggling to let any sound through. 'I left them outside Buckley's'

Remnants of her childhood athleticism were reconnected by sheer adrenaline as she dashed across the cruel gravel drive in bare feet, down the road and around into the Park Hall Road row of shops. Vanessa was still asleep but John awake and feeling peckish had devoured a substantial amount of raw mincemeat. It was several years before we had a similar life shortening experience.

Chapter 6

Elephant in the Bendix, Tiger in the Tank.

Jane was a sweet natured nervous four-year-old who said little. She had taken some time to settle into nursery school and would rather have been at home amusing John and practicing her mothering skills on Vanessa. Jane's birth had coincided with a father having prolonged intensive rehabilitation from life threatening polio and a mother who needed to complete her clinical placements to allow her to practice medicine to take on the support of the family. Jane's early daily care was undertaken by the then 'mother's help' Audrey who having started the job with one baby, had a second, and not long after Jane's third birthday, got pregnant for a third time. By mutual agreement it was decided that she would be unable to cope with the workload created by the children *and* a pig-headed house bound polio victim so returned to live with her father.

Until I had turned up a succession of home helps came and left in the previous year for a variety of reasons. Peter having declined all mechanical help ranging from an iron lung to a walking stick was back on his feet with the aid of a leg iron by the time Jane was a year old. They both spent months learning to walk, she, mastering the art quicker than he did. With the other children at school he studied for the Diploma in Psychiatry she learned that quietness pleased him when he was busy and that she would be rewarded by his attention when he was not. At nap time, she was content to sleep near him on the floor usually in a position that prevented him from getting out of his chair by the kitchen Aga. Jane had chosen to curl around his feet like a cat so was fast asleep when one day the Bendix took on a life of its own. The contents, which had contained a much-loved stuffed elephant, became a solid ball when the spin started rattling the drum from side to side This problem is usually resolved by stopping the machine, over-riding the door opening mechanism, untangling the contents and restarting the spin. To give Peter his due he was familiar enough with this procedure but a combination of a very weak right leg and child entrapment had

him in the path of a berserk Bendix which had abandoned its side to side rocking and was now creeping forward, attached water pipes straining to achieve its purpose which seemed to be to crush the sleeping child and incapacitated father. The Bendix came within inches of achieving it aim. It was only balked by the power point being wrenched from its socket by the march of the megaton.
Jane at some point woke to the mayhem which now included cold water gushing from the wrenched off cold water inlet.

When Peter was relaying this story to me I was not interested in the subsequent clear up merely seeking an explanation as to why Jane wouldn't stay in the kitchen alone if the Bendix was on, and to find out why Dumbo the Elephant had been naughty?
'Well', he said shiftily 'I thought if I blamed Dumbo she would not be afraid of the machine because we could promise not to wash him in the Bendix again'.
So, was that why there was a poor neglected grubby floppy eared elephant in the toy box?
Were there any more bogeyman stories I should know about?
'Well, you may have noticed that Mark never pulls the chain in the loo'
Yes...?
'Well he thinks there's a tiger in the tank.
'Ok…?
'And there's Billy Goat Gruff'. 'My Spy' he added as if that made it all right.
'Oh and, there's The Macking Ram the elusive 'Mr. Nobody' who gets the blame for everything' he continued, and then added as an afterthought.
'And of course there's Claud the Terrible, but he's in Sussex'… 'Now he really is a Bogeyman' he said with feeling.
Jezzis wept! A couple of lines from an old nursery line came to mind
'Here comes the Bogeyman dressed in black
Carrying children in his sack'

I was fast coming to the conclusion that psychiatrists, like psychopaths, should not be allowed to procreate.

Chapter 7

Morning has broken.

A month or so into life in Dulwich and my days were in an established twelve hourly routine. Nurse training had prepared me for early rising and motherhood for broken nights so although the hours were long the work was not arduous and with a young baby in tow, my gadding about was restricted anyway. I was free to entertain friends if I wanted to but tho' some undertook the long trek from East London initially, few repeated it. While they blamed the journey, I think it was more likely to be the penetrating and excruciatingly frank interrogation from Simon, Mark and Emma, the silent intimidating scrutiny of Jane, the drooling of a teething baby or the projectile regurgitation of an even smaller one down their best frocks. While I rescued Ann and Peter's guests after ten minutes of 'meet the children' they never returned the favour when I entertained nor made any attempt to be responsible for their children's usual bed time routines.

The kitchen calendar, courtesy of Park Hall Pharmacy, soon filled up with events accommodating the children's social life, games fixtures, class assemblies, birthday parties and swimming, all with an initial A, B, or P next to the entries. Take a guess as to which initial appeared most frequently? My organisational skills were stretched to the limit. A daily routine was now established and began the night before when Peter or Ann laid the table for breakfast after they had cleared up after dinner. Pre-setting a table was a new notion for them as was joining their children for breakfast. I was usually woken at 6.00am by Vanessa wanting a feed, shortly followed by John who always chose early morning for a mega bowel movement. A clean up and a drink of water sent him dozing off again. I had taught Jane not to get out of bed until the big hand was on six and the little hand was on seven but she was still coping with the intricacies of donning a school uniform so was always awake before her 7.30 alarm. Since I had learned to grind coffee and make it the way he liked it Peter now joined his children at the table long enough to drink a cup, crunch a piece of toast, and read the

Guardian headlines. Ann, too, braved what had previously been a time of unfettered anarchy and joined four uniform clad courteous children at 8.00am.

Anybody looking in on the scene would find it heart-warming. However, if the Peeping Tom had hung around for the transit from the feeding station to their dispatch to school a different story would emerge. In anticipation of this ritual both parents would disappear into thin air. Sometimes I would be quick enough to see a whiff of exhaust as a pale blue Anglia slid through the gateposts or the sitting room closing quietly as Ann sought the sanctuary of her office. I think it was Nancy Mitford who said 'Children's voices are so boring because the bore right through your head' if it wasn't her it was somebody wise in the ways of children. She definitely said 'I love children, especially when they cry, for then someone takes them away'. In this situation, I was the one who had been given the rough end of the pineapple. My grandmother used to say of my mother 'That woman (no love lost) would be a lot happier with a lady's maid and a full-time Nanny', well so would Ann, but her financial situation and feminist leanings precluded that luxury. However, employing an unmarried mothers help, a char and lady 'wot does' gave her street cred among her friends in the Socialist elite and fulfilled the functions of the former for a fraction of the cost.

Every morning as I mustered the children to get them out the door to school there would be a repeat of the following exchanges with minor irritating variations;

Me; 'Anybody got games today (noting that nobody is clutching a kit bag)'?

At least one child runs to get kit.

Me; Ok everybody, have you all brushed your teeth?

Jane nods.

Emma displays teeth.

Mark; 'I can't, Simon cleaned his rugger boots with my toothbrush'.

Simon; 'You're a liar. I used it to clean pigeon poo off the window'.

Pause to separate Simon and Mark.

Me; Ok have you all combed your hair?

Simon removes a practically toothless comb from blazer pocket and makes an impotent attempt at tangled mop.

Me; I stick Simon's head under cloakroom tap. He complains that water is too hot/ too cold/ that I've wet his shirt collar/blazer. Realise he has nits.

Emma; 'You broke my brush when you whacked me'.

Me 'Well use your comb'

Me; 'Mark, where's your jumper, you'll need it'?

Simon smirking, 'No he won't, he's got playtime detention.

Mark glaring at Simon, 'Tell-tale tit'.

Pause to separate Mark and Simon.

Me; 'If you've got detention you must have been given a note'?

Mark, 'It's only a playtime detention not a real detention (by way of mitigation) producing a crumpled hand written note stamped with teachers name from his schoolbag. Note explains playtime detention for fighting and appeals for the return of permission slip to allow him to join his class on a museum trip.

Me; Search school bag and find permission slip. Also, find matchbox with lettuce leaf and caterpillar. Forge mother's signature on permission slip.

Mark. 'That's illegal'.

Me; Do *you* want to explain to your mother? (Thought not!)

Me; 'Has anybody else got a note from school'? Simon?

Simon. 'Nope'.

Mark. 'Yes he has'

Pause to separate Simon and Mark

Simon (by way of clarification) 'It's not a note it's a letter' (why are children *so* pedantic?)

(NB Explanation for grown up pedants; a written note is from a teacher, a typed letter with headed paper, is from the Head's Office and therefore OFFICIAL.)

 Read letter requesting the pleasure of the said child's parents in Headmasters study that very afternoon?

Simon sent to give the letter to mother but keeps walking.

Carpool mother's child is at the door for Emma and Jane.

Me; 'Ok off you go'

Emma; Scowls at child and glares accusingly at me and in her 'it's not f-a-i-r tone of voice' shouts with righteous indignation

'Why do you make me brush my teeth when you don't make Peter brush his'?

Hmm, good point, but I have learned to speak 'child' and not to get side tracked so kept such dialectic battles and debates for the delights of bed time.

For those of you versed in the circumlocutions of what passes for children's minds you will know that while adults make statements children make questions, and first thing in the morning is not a good time to take them on. Before you know it, your voice is raising in line with your blood pressure.

Jane, (removing her satchel and blazer) 'I need to do a poopee…

Me. 'Suffering Jezzis' (heartfelt and under breath) then;

Apologise to stony faced mother in Volvo Amazon Wagon.

Check that Mark makes it through the gates of Prep School opposite.

Wait for absconder to reappear because I sure as hell am not telling his mother.

Anticipate a tense evening.

Buy a nit comb.

Chapter 8

Many shades of grey.

On school days when the hall door closed on the children it was as if the whole house gave a sigh of relief. It was now time for babies, clearing up, putting on a wash, shopping, hanging out clothes, putting on a wash, getting lunch ready, hanging out clothes, putting on a wash, putting babies down for afternoon nap, putting feet up to read paper, hanging out clothes, preparing tea for children's return from school. At some time in the early months this shorthand way depicting the children was used. Years hence, and with another baby, we were still using this demarcation despite the three 'Babies' objections.

Washing for a large family was an endless chore as was hanging it all up to dry. It was made more onerous in an era were Harrington terry nappies lined with muslin squares were in vogue. Buckets of nappies soaking in Milton constantly sat by the Bendix awaiting their turn. How did my Aunt May in Galway manage a mega wash for a family of nine every Monday? She had no running water, or washing machine, just a washboard, Sunlight soap, Reckitt's blue and a mangle. Like any farmer's wife her routine was

Wash on Monday
Iron on Tuesday
Bake on Wednesday
Scrub on Thursday
Churn on Friday
Shrive on Saturday
Mass on Sunday'

Coming from a stratum of society that appreciated a washing line of white nappies I had to stop Ann 'helping out' with packing the Bendix because it had taken me weeks to get the sludge tones out of sheets. Dark green towels and navy and blue banded rugger shirts did not enhance white underwear or shorts. Luckily Simon's and Mark's uniform consisted of grey shorts, grey shirts, grey jumpers and grey knee length socks. On the other hand, Emma and Jane's uniform was a white and red striped dress in summer; with grey skirt, white blouse and red cardigan in winter. However, the bane of my life was their white knee length socks. A tinge of grey threw Emma into flouncing rages, but this was as nothing compared to Simons fuss if his underwear was returned to him with a hint of pink. The day that John's zip-up raspberry red pram suit inadvertently got into a 'white' wash was one to remember. I could understand now why Peter insisted on the luxury of sending shirts and underwear out to the local laundry.

Ann had a 'thing' about bibs. I regarded them as labour saving; she considered them as something a slattern would use to reduce the amount of times baby's clothes were changed.

So, I was a slattern. So, what?

With one drooling baby, one puking baby and a finite amount of baby clothes when she removed a bib, I replaced it. This went on until the incident of the button. John had never been allowed a dummy and had not yet learned to suck his thumb so to satisfy his need for oral gratification he took to sucking on cardigan buttons and the tabs of zips. Without a bib, he had free range so a regular trawl through his poo became necessary when a button went missing. On this occasion, it was a particularly nice filigree silver bauble from a German Fair Isle type cardigan which, when shaken, made the sound of a miniature bell. It failed to re-appear. We tried shaking him to see if we could hear it, but rattling a reluctant 16lb baby was no easy matter. His bellowing would have cloaked the noise of complete orchestral tambourine and tympani sections. There was nothing for it but to take him to the Westminster Children's Hospital for an x-ray. This was not our nearest hospital but Peter being a member of staff in the Psychiatric Dept. meant we jumped the queue. No sign of the button was found but Ann ceased removing bibs.

Several weeks later I saw Jane playing with her ribbon box. Jane, whose hair was short, dark and curly, collected ribbons but never wore them; although they sometimes adorned her dolls. Nestling in the box was the missing bauble. 'Where did this come from' I asked? She clasped it in her hand as if she would never see it again.

'I bit it off John's cardigan' she whispered.

'You'll find five more in the button box' I informed her as her face lit up

Not taking any chances I had exchanged them for buttons that would traverse a seven months old intestinal tract. When I told Peter, his response was 'Bloody Krauts, they're trying to get their own back for Dresden'. Peter never learned political correctness. In years to come his tolerance was severely tested by Kraut and Frog exchange students who came to stay. Having seen service out in the Pacific in his Navy days he wouldn't buy 'Nip' goods but he did eventually succumb to the high-end technology of a Grundig music centre.

Chapter 9

Knock-knock, who's there?

School got out at 3.30 but arrival home time was dependent on detention, games or afterschool clubs. Like homing pigeons, they came through the backdoor in dribs and drabs I provided them with a drink and a snack to sustain them until tea at 5.00. To prevent whinging and cries of unfairness the snack was set out on separate plates but this did not prevent Simon from attempting to scoff the lot. He had also by now taken to raiding the babies' Farley's Rusk supply. The children amused themselves until the tea was ready to dish up. Emma settled down to homework, Jane to playing with the babies' and Mark and Simon to squabbling. Ann joined us for tea making an effort to be available to the children for an hour or so, however she could never resist a ringing phone so tea time often found her meandering back to her desk leaving me with disgruntled children to amuse.

Bed times were staggered between 7.00 pm and 8.00 pm and it was by far the most exhausting hour of the day. John and Vanessa were no bother. Bathed and fed they went straight off to sleep with Jane soon following them happy with a story and a slice of apple. Descending to the first floor and a bathroom awash with water from Emma and Simons ablutions I would have to wrestle Mark into submission to wash his neck and ears. The problem with the older children's bed time was that Peter got home about 7.00 and Simon and Mark would take on a new lease of life vying for his attention. When they started quarrelling, as they inevitably did, he would walk away and close the study door on them. In retaliation, they would try to provoke him into grabbing them to give them a wallop but they were far too fast for his lack of mobility so they usually got a swat from me in passing instead. Emma opted for her mother's attention while she prepared dinner. She craved individual consideration and affection but had to fight hard for it. It was tough for her to gain approval when the boys were always in competition. Their provoking behaviour got an inevitable reaction which usually resulted in all three being shooed from the kitchen. So, recognition and reward for good behaviour often fell by the wayside to be replaced with disappointment on her part and irritability on her mothers whose 'terms of engagement' did not include dealing with squabbling children.

To complete my twelve-hour day, I was supposed to see to it that the children went to bed at their allotted time while they're parents enjoyed a quiet, uninterrupted meal.

Easier said than done.

Children are very forgiving so whatever our shouting matches during the day they were more than willing to let bygones be bygones when it came to bedtime rituals.

Procrastination was the name of the game. For those of you ignorant of the rules they are as follows;

Questions,
Announcements,
Debate,
Defence,
Coup de grâce,
Farwell appearance
Final word.

Note to readers and 'yes, but' parents;

Before battle commences it is important to make a firm resolve not to lose concentration by becoming distracted or, or worst still, side-tracked, and if you have girded your loins by imbibing a stiff gin and tonic *never ever make a mellow non-committal 'uh hu' response.* It will be either taken as a 'yes', or as a subject open to negotiation or debate.

Questions;
'Have you washed my games kit'?
'Have I got any clean socks (gazing at heap of clothes on floor)
'Can I have a parrot' (guess who?)
'Why are you always so horrible'?
Announcements;
'I've left my PE kit in Alexander's house'

'I've left my bike out in the rain'

''My rugger boots are too small'

'I've lost my swimming trunks'

I can't find my Lacrosse stick'

'I think my lizard is dying' (guess who?)

'I need'……....................

Items varied from the ridiculous to the impossible and more often than not could only be supplied with the aid of a magic wand or a prayer to St. Jude, Patron Saint of lost causes. However, I did manage a pair of fluffy rabbit ears overnight for Jane's Easter Bunny school pageant.

Debate;

Why? What for? How come?

It's not f-a-i-r.

'You're not in charge of me'

'Stephanie's mummy lets her stay up to watch' …

Defence;

'Because I said so'!

'Because I said so'!

'Because I said so'!

Coup de grâce;

'If you don't get into bed I'll murder the whole bloody lot of you'.

Farewell appearance;

'I forgot to brush my teeth'

'I need a drink of water'

'Wanna hear a joke'?

Final word;

'Wanna whack'?

I was beginning to learn what it would be like if children ruled the world.

If boys were in charge

You would never have to wash your neck and ears.

You would never have to change your clothes, brush your teeth or comb your hair.

You would never have to flush the loo or put the seat down.

You could eat chocolate and ice-cream whenever you like.

You could have as many pets as you wanted.

There would be no homework, bedtime and no dirty rugger boots to clean.

There would be no stupid school rules, detention, caning, games on wet days, or communal showers.

There would be no bossy sisters but if there were, you could punch them.

On the other hand, if girls ruled the world;

You could use as much bubble bath as you like.

You would have a personal maid to change your clothes, put the toothpaste on your tooth brush and dress your hair trice daily.

You would have your own toilet and bath cleaned by your personal maid.

You could eat as much chocolate and ice-cream as you like, surreptitiously.

You would have a pony in the back garden and a groom to shovel shit.

There would be no homework, or bedtime and lacrosse shoes would be cleaned by personal maid.

There would be a magic elixir for early morning grumpiness as a result of sleep deprivation.

There would be no obnoxious brothers but if there were you could scream at them.

Time 8.00pm and the rest of the evening is my own apart from lights out. The oldest three were encouraged to read in bed in the hope that they would fall asleep doing so, and this worked a treat with Simon and Mark. It had the opposite effect on Emma, firing her imagination and a need to read 'just one more chapter'. She could have read all night as far as I was concerned if her late nights had not affected the whole household the following morning. Her irritability and grumpiness often ended in screams, tears, flouncing and a lot door banging on the way out to school. A parents meeting with Emma's Head of Year brought matters to a head.

'She has got to go to sleep earlier' Ann pontificated knowing she was not qualified to impose this boundary, so the compliance problem became mine. There then followed a period of futile conflict between Emma and me which was only resolved when a change in her circadian rhythm at puberty solved the problem and she became a morning person. It was no surprise to hear her interest in literature has become a career.

Chapter 10

Sunday, bloody Sundays.

Theoretically Sunday was my day off but unless I was prepared to lock myself in my room, or go out for the day, the children ignored the fact and Ann and Peter paid it lip service. John still woke at 7.00 and needed his nappy changed. Jane still made her silent appearance. I had started using the upstairs kitchen for Sunday breakfast so we would have it in peace while listening to the bellowing and shouting downstairs. Emma escaped to Sussex most weekends travelling alone with a tip to the Guard to make sure she got off at Pulborough where she was picked up by Barbara, so it mostly Mark and Simon winding each other up with the expected reaction from their parents. Impotent threats from Peter, towering rage from Ann. As soon as silence descended I knew that the boys would be taking the opportunity to get into mischief while Peter and Ann would be attempting a trawl through the Sunday papers. Ann at the time was writing a book called the A to Z of Babies and like other child care gurus of the era theorised that children must be respected, have their egos nurtured and feelings considered. These experts, mostly male, either didn't have children, or if they did, farmed them out to be psychoanalyzed or had wives and nannies to raise them, and like Ann, probably seldom spent more than an hour a day in their company.

Less financially endowed parents, stuck with rearing their children 24hrs a day, and who were available to be loved, hated and relied upon knew that they were not dealing with mini adults but with a foreign species of anarchic savages, who were without morals or scruples, and who, given the opportunity, would, like a shoal of piranha's, eat each other. Like me they would have loved to see their children's childhood being enriched by warm and tender memories of peace, harmony and reasoned negotiation instead of their darling offspring being marshalled and chivvied along by a string of directives, or being cowed into submission by the occasional well deserved whack and threats of further punishment or a violent death.

The latter brings to mind a childhood memory of a desperate neighbour in Dublin. Reaching the end of her endurance May Donoghue, walked her children across to the nearby Royal Canal and drowned herself and all six children. For years afterwards, May was used as a yardstick to gauge somebody's state of mind coping with the stress and strife of raising children in poor circumstances. 'Well' things are bad, but I'm not as desperate as poor May' neighbours would say. Or when their children were scourging them; 'Suffering Jesus, if youze don't get out from under me feet I'll take youze all down to the feckin canal and drown yez' Depression was regarded as a luxury the poor couldn't afford, but an attack of nerves or a 'touch of the nagers' as it was euphemistically called was accepted. Mental illness was poorly understood but if a mother had a 'touch of the nagers' or was feeling melancholic, neighbours rallied around and offered the family what support they could until she was able to face the world again. Support for men with the nagers was more judgemental because it usually went hand in hand with 'the drink' and family strife.

The first time Jane instigated a voluntary conversation with me was on a Sunday morning. Everything was peace and quiet downstairs which had my antenna twitching. A united Simon and Mark were ten times more dangerous than a squabbling pair so while I was tempted to find out what they were up to, I was equally determined not to interfere. I was enlightened obliquely by Jane. Looking down on the garden she announced

'The gardens on fire'.

She was right, the distant third of the garden, which was little more than a jungle was belching smoke. With two babies' playing on the floor I was stuck. Shouting over the banisters to Peter and Ann proved futile so I sent Jane down. I expected an instant response but nothing happened. I closed the bedroom door on John and Vanessa to prevent them toppling down the stairs. I found the ever-obedient Jane standing knocking on the sitting door waiting to be told to come in. She hadn't a chance against the majesty of *Die Walküre*.

I usually joined the family for Sunday lunch which was anytime between 1.00 ~ 2.00 depending on when Ann remembered to put the roast in the oven. It was now normally a fairly civilised meal and one at which Peter presided. A few whinges about the meagre amount of roast potatoes, and a Yuk from the 'I hate broccoli' brigade and a bowlful of untouched salad were minor irritants. After lunch one parent or the other would have the children for an hour or so, Ann choosing the Horniman Museum familiarly known as the 'Dead Zoo' or Crystal Palace Swimming Pool leaving Peter to choose between Dulwich Park duck feeding, sitting in the playroom rocking chair adjudicating on a chest tournament between Simon and Mark or more likely lying on the floor playing with the Scalextric. For those of you who never had a Scalextric set it consisted of a powered track with two slots on which small model cars could be guided around the track. As time passed we accumulated a massive track with chicanes and overpasses. There was no need to steer, all the user of Scalextric had to do was place the car in the grooves, pull the trigger on the handset to make the car go faster, and release it a little for the car to slow down at corners. Two cars raced at a time, however with four handsets a game of carnage was possible and always ended in tears or sulks, tears from the children, sulks from somebody who should have known better.

Jane's favourite Sunday afternoon activity was sitting on Peter's lap reading her well-thumbed much loved sticky copy of 'The Cat in the Hat'. I looked after John until tea time bringing him down to Ann to have some time with him until bed time. I enjoyed a quiet tea upstairs and spent a peaceful few hours with Vanessa. Theoretically the children's Sunday bed time was none of my business but it was I who would have to face the Monday morning chaos and listen to Ann's rising impatience as they went through their usual bedtime diversionary tactics.

Hmm… whatever happened to her oft expressed philosophy of reasoned negotiation when dealing with children? To give her due she seldom resorted to the *because I said so* cop out, or a well-deserved slap, so consequently Simon and Mark could bring her to a door banging shouting fury. They knew that trying those tactics with me could lead to dire consequences. Chip, pancakes, flapjacks and fudge deprivation could be a very painful experience especially if you had to watch your siblings devouring your portion.

Time 8.00 pm; where had, the day gone? Perhaps I'll go to Mass next Sunday?

Chapter 11

The Bogey Man.

Mid-April and an overfilled Bedford van, suspension groaning and full of children and belongings saw us on our way to Graffham in West Sussex the home of Opa and Oma, Ann's parents. It was Good Friday and we would be spending the Easter holidays with them. We had to leave the twin pram behind but Ann assured me that there was a plethora of childhood equipment in the old nursery which had come with the family when they moved there in 1948. I had assumed she meant from *her* childhood not her mothers, however I found an ancient bucket pram which, with a good scouring and stuffed with old pillows made a passable carriage for two for the week. Coming in on the road from Petworth the first glimpse of Glasses as we turned into the drive was a small gate house on the right where the gardener and daily help lived and Barbara's house, Weavers Cottage on the left. A curve in the tree lined drive hid the house from the road and we had to progress up a noticeable incline before we caught a glimpse of it and its sweeping lawns and grounds. It was a lovely picture postcard residence built for the gentry at the turn of the century. Eight bedrooms, three bathrooms and three reception rooms makes it sound commodious but with nine of us it was a bit of a squeeze. The surrounding land had obviously served as a farm at some point because behind Barbara's cottage was a converted barn, and a long low cattle shed that had been converted into a craft and weaving centre by Oma. At the far side of the house, on level ground, was a neglected tennis court, a kitchen garden and chicken run.

On the journey down Ann had given me a potted history of her father and his intolerance of noisy, unruly children.

Hmm, this was going to be a fun filled week!

She issued dire warnings to the children that there would be no pocket money if they annoyed Opa. I knew this was an idle threat since she would cave in by Saturday so I suggested, much to the children's delight, that they could earn extra pocket money by observing rules that would avoid upsetting him. This discussion shortened the journey as the children refined the rules to ensure maximum reward. We ended up with the following six

'DO NOTS'.

Do not play in the front hall (where his study was)

Do not play outside his study window

Do not use the front entrance (which took them past his study)

Do not use the cloakroom inside the front door (it was his personal loo)

Never use the upstairs corridor to his and Oma' bedrooms

Never ever jump down the stairs by his study because the satisfying thuds on landing sent him in to towering rages.

The children's amount of weekly pocket money was graded by age, Simon's rate being a shilling, Mark 10d, Emma 8d and Jane 6d; however, the rules under debate put the same onus on everybody to behave so it was only fair that everybody was rewarded equally. It took from Godolming to Petworth to persuade Simon of the justice of this. The reward would be an individual shilling for everybody if they avoided annoying Opa.

Would coughing or sneezing count?

What about farting?

It was decreed that involuntary noises would count if they annoyed him because you were obviously somewhere you shouldn't be. I can't remember the study of semantics that followed on the meaning of the Verb 'to annoy'; however, when it happened nobody was left in any doubt that Opa was annoyed.

Oma was a charming and cultured woman in her late fifties and seventeen years younger than her husband. An heiress from a family of well-established merchant bankers she had the courtesy and assurance that comes with money, and the breeding that comes with old money. Her grandchildren loved her and she tolerated a lot of their boisterous behaviour around the house and grounds on the understanding that they kept out of sight and sound of their Grandfather. This was relatively easy if the little darlings kept to the back of the house. With back and side entrances and an old nursery wing to ourselves we had no reason to even meet Opa since he sure as hell wasn't going to choose to eat with us. The only place I might run in to him was the kitchen in the unlikely event that he entered it. When we had settled in Oma came to find me in the commodious kitchen where I was preparing a meal for the children. Although I had spoken to her several times on the telephone this was the first time we had met so we exchanged quite a lot of information including the rewards for good behaviour for the week. She didn't exactly say 'Talk of the Devil'… but she said

'I think you should meet Claud before he comes upon you unexpectedly'.

'Why, what would he do' (I was tempted to ask)?

She knocked on his study door and waited for a response. She repeated the knock before there was a thunderous and abrupt

'Come'.

We entered as he swivelled around from his desk his half-moon glasses well down his nose. He glared at us. If it had been just me I might have taken it personally. He was a tall angular featured ungainly looking man whom my nursing eye noted had the prominent jaw and large hands and feet of somebody who had had pituitary problems.

'Claud, this is Bernadette, Ann's new Nanny' she informed him.

Ah, I had gone up in the world!

I held his gaze as he looked me up and down as if sifting through my brain for signs of degeneracy. Finding nothing of consequence he decided to turn on the full beam of his charm. I realised he must have been an attractive man in his prime because even in his mid-seventies he had the power to seduce. With me the charm was adjusted to half beam when he realised I was Irish but I couldn't fault his agreeableness.

It must have been galling for him to have a surname one would assume was of Irish origin, but instead of coming from across the Irish Sea his ancestors were hoary handed sons of the soil from Wilshire. Having been dreading meeting The Bogey Man I was as astonished as Oma to find him in a benevolent mood and I was delighted to have established a good rapport. Ann was as doubting as Thomas when Oma relayed the encounter. Her teenage tempestuous relationship with him had scarred their interaction thereafter, and his disapproval and intolerance of her 'horde' of children while ignoring her academic accomplishments was galling for her. None of this family history was any of my business all I had to do was to make sure the children earned their reward. Those of you who have read my previous memoirs will know that I am cursed, and that there was no way on the God's good earth that this was going to happen.

Chapter 12

Malevolence and vitriol.

Easter Saturday was uneventful with Mark and Simon spending most of searching for the stash of Easter eggs they believed I had. To keep them away from their grandfather I assured them the eggs were not in the house. This was in fact true since I had put them in the boot of Peter's car for him to bring down later that evening. He was only staying for two nights, his tolerance for socialising being about 4 degrees above zero. On a road where you were more likely to meet a horse than a motor we all took a nice slow amble up to the village shop. Four children selecting sweets with as many as five for a penny took considerable time, but to the shop keeper local children were a valued source of revenue and not to be rushed. John, with only a penny to spend was old enough now to suck a lolly and had a choice of red, purple, orange, yellow or green and couldn't understand why he couldn't have all five. Jane, ever generous treated Vanessa to a dab of her sherbet lemon which opened her eyes in surprise and irritated her sinuses into an outburst of prolonged sneezing.

Peter's arrival, by an irrational route via Piccadilly which he always chose (orienteering was not his strong point), was greeted with unconfined pleasure and for once an evening of unusual harmony was had by all, even Peter, sedated by a surfeit of Claud's best Claret. He arranged with me to have Jane up and dressed early so that she could go around the grounds with him and Oma hiding the contents of a large box of miniature Easter eggs for the hunt. This would even up her chances of finding some and also gave her time with him. He had a soft spot for Jane developed on their long days spent together during his recuperation. Each child would also receive a large chocolate egg but those would not be distributed until after lunch in the hope that they would eat some of the splendid meal Oma and I would be preparing. I was trying to keep them corralled in the kitchen so that they couldn't spy on the egg hiding trio when Peter walked in with the empty box indicating the hunt would be on as soon as Jane had been to the loo, but pure Darwinism took over and the three scavengers were out the door. Ann followed with John and Vanessa in the pram to ensure that nobody took the survival of the fittest to its logical conclusion.

At the same time bellows of rage came from the front hall. I dashed from the kitchen to find Claud in meltdown shouting and battering the door of the cloakroom, teeth gnashing like a deranged Barbary Macaque. Holy Mother of God, Jane must be in there. Now what Claud didn't know was that I was well seasoned in dealing with character forming bullies and that apart from his roar he was no physical match for me. I might get a crack of his cane before I was able to wrest it from him, but despite his size, with an adrenaline rush I could lay him out without too much trouble, probably killing him in the progress. I gave him 'The Look' I sometimes had to use to shrivel children and let him rant until he was blue in the face. Eventually he drew breath so I said 'Go away and let me get her out'. I choked on the word 'Sir' and just couldn't bring myself to say it. I didn't know whether he was by then dancing with rage or because his bladder was going to burst, either way I knew that getting Jane out was going to take some time so I advised him to find another loo. I thought he was going to strike me but despite his truly monumental rage some vestige of his legal training remained, that, and a glimpse of Peter coming to the rescue and he shuffled off.

It took all of Peter's cajoling and assurance and my reminding her that the Easter egg hunt was in progress before she pulled back the bolt. The pair of them went off to join the hunt and I headed to the kitchen to get on with the lunch. I heard Claud before I saw him. He had his back to me and was telling his version of the story to Oma who could see me entering the kitchen.

'I want that Papist, Fenian, Whore out of this house right now' he commanded foaming at the mouth.

Coming from a former Barrister at Law and Stipendiary Magistrate these accusations were strong stuff and factually inaccurate and would see me adequately recompensed in a civil court. I was tempted to debate the semantics involved with him but realised the greater power of silence contempt. Where had, the charming urbane host gone? Oma looked mortified but when I took no notice of him she appeared relieved and followed my example by ignoring him and joined me at the sink. When he had turned on his heel and walked out she said

'I'm sorry my dear but Claud can be a very unpleasant man at times, you did well to ignore him'.

'So, I take it I'm not being banished from the house then' I asked mischievously?

'Good heavens no, you're well able to take care of yourself, as for Claud, *he'll* have to look out for *himself*' she said with a laugh.

My one regret was that at teatime I told Peter what Claud had said. I had forgotten that Peter had been a Lieutenant in the Royal Navy so had probably learned his choice vocabulary there. He never raised his voice but he had a way of clamping his jaw and hardening his eyes that usually put the children on alert not to cross the line. I knew when he got up from the table that he was heading for Claud's study and tried to dissuade him. 'I'm not having him speak to you like that, nor am I going to let the arrogant prick terrorise my children' he said through teeth clenched in fury. I didn't want Claud to think I had gone running to Peter for his protection. I wanted him to know that he would take me on at his peril. I never found out what transpired but it was noticeable that Peter now only came down when Claud was not in residence. For two weeks, every spring Claud took himself off on a Cruise, usually heading for the Greek Archipelago. This lifted everybody's spirits including his own.

Jane had recovered by bed time and was lamenting to Peter that she had lost out on her *Do Not Annoy Opa* reward.

'No, no, no' he told her. Billy (his Secret Agent) had told him it was Bernadette who had annoyed Opa so *she* should be punished by giving Jane her Easter egg.

By the end of the week all the children had earned their reward with me turning a deaf ear to the thuds following the irresistible urge to jump the last few stairs outside his study.

During my exploration of Oma's attics, I came across a practically unused treadle sewing machine which she was happy for me to take back to Dulwich, and so making and altering clothes was added to my attempts at frugality.

Chapter 13

'What part of NO don't you understand'?

The month of May found Peter's parent's visiting from Plymouth. Pops, an ex-Royal Navy Dental Surgeon and Nan were two nice middle class people somewhat in awe of Peter and his professional wife. Peter had followed his father into the Royal Navy. Pops in turn had followed another three generations of Welsh shipwrights into the Naval Yards, an alternative to working in the coal mines. The children were pleased to see them but tried to get away with murder in the hope that I would turn a blind eye to their transgressions. 'Beds are for sleeping in, not jumping on' fell on deaf ears until Marks bed collapsed. Nan, whom Pops called Mac was a bit ditzy, forgetful and apologetic which she made up for by her cheerfulness and willing to be the butt of the Mr. Nobody joke. It was on this visit that I learned her family name was Ingram and her given names Mary Alice Constance shortened to Mac, which when punned was the 'Macking Ram'. Pop's taught Mark to make annoying noises with a blade of grass held lengthwise between his thumbs. He also traversed the garden with him on wildlife hunts with both of them under a sentence of death and eternal damnation if they brought anything into the house. Lily had already given notice twice having come across a nest of woodlice and an enormous spider. Mark's response was one of total indignation 'She has no business opening boxes and tins' he said with some justification, and while I agreed with him I was not about to sacrifice Lily's help. I was the only one with search and seizure rights so I had a word with her. Apart from dinner with Peter and Ann it fell to me to entertain his parents.

Their stay coincided with Vanessa's christening, a memorable day for several reasons. The children, pagans all, had never been in a church before so full of curiosity they set out to explore while we, the adults, gathered around the Baptismal Font. In an otherwise empty church the penetrating childish voices echoed from the gallery to the sacristy as the ceremony got underway. Vanessa had progressed to pureed food in an effort to reduce her regurgitation problem. A useless attempt at a solution because when tipped up by the priest after her sprinkling with water his surplice was showered by a projectile vomit of putrid semi digested Heinz Steamed Fish that would make a hog gag. A vision of a baby named Fred on the Paediatric Ward at St. Andrews whose spectacular and effortless regurgitation of four ounces of National Dried over the head of the Consultant materialised before my eyes as the Rev practically threw Vanessa at her godmother, Leila, who nearly dropped her as she joined in his desire to puke.

Peter too couldn't deal with puke and turned green. He couldn't even deal with gagging. As a medical student, he had to take early morning gastric fluid samples from patients with suspected ulcers. This was achieved by passing a nasogastric tube up a fasting patient's nose down into the stomach making them retch as it passed through the oesophagus. Doing this under the supervision of a fierce beady eyed night sister he disgraced himself by filling the vomit bowl she was holding with his own 'morning after the night before' stomach contents when the patient began to gag.

Vanessa had also managed to cover the Redmond family heirloom christening gown in her copious upchuck. The reason there are no photographs of the less than solemn occasion is that Peter, fighting his desire to puke, forgot to take the lens cover off the camera. I handed over the envelope with the agreed remuneration to the Rev, and gathering up the children we made our way back to the house for a small celebration. Simon and Mark disappeared down to the bottom of the garden in their 'best of buddies' mode. Peter was just as suspicious as I was so followed them down to find out what heinous crime they were committing and found them emptying the church Poor Box. They had robbed the House of God... and why not?

We were poor, weren't we?

Finders keepers and all that?

After all the box was just sitting there on a table?

I have never seen Peter move so fast. He had the pair of them back at the Rectory before the theft had been discovered otherwise we would have has an even more memorable day involving blue flashing lights.

Please note when the church was razed to the ground we had long moved. However, it wasn't our last encounter with a Vicar.

Chapter 14

'I don't care who started it'.

Fights between Simon and Mark were still a tedious and a recurrent happening. My daily measure of success was that when Ann and Peter came home at night that they would find their children still alive, but by half term in May I had had enough of the pair of them trying to obliterate each other so one day after lunch I threw them out in the garden and left them to it. Normally Ann or I would go out and separate them after half an hour or so but on this occasion Ann was at the BBC discussing the possibility of recording a series of radio programmes and was not expected back much before 5.00pm. I decided that they could fight to the death or resolve their rivalry once and for all. I could not understand how one of them could infuriate the other to the point when a red mist descended. Although there was only a fifteen-month age gap, on the face of it, they were not in direct competition with each other, but sibling rivalry is a story as old as mankind: Cain and Abel started it, Romulus and Remus followed and Simon and Mark were keeping it going.

Simon was gregarious, charismatic and a bit of a chancer in that he would try to charm his way out of retribution by lying smoothly and shamelessly. He paid lip service to authority, but although he was ambitious, if a school subject did not interest him, he would not hide his lack of motivation so got more than his fair share of detentions. He hated games but did quite well at cricket if he could be trusted not to loll about in the long grass. Languages came easily to him but his scatter-brained approach kept him from shining.

Mark was the exact opposite in many ways. He was more competitive, taciturn, honest, curious and never denied wrongdoing. He kept out of trouble at school, focussing on his lessons, and was a tenacious team player at games and a star at PE. Simon's ease with languages may have irked Mark but it could also be to his advantage if he could learn to co-operate with his brother during homework time.

Not many punches were ever exchanged during these 'fights'. They quickly degenerated into wrestling matches which started with energetic throws then holds of some complexity; half Nelson, bear hug, body press, chin and head locks and head scissors. Until now they had never perfected finishing moves because they had always been separated issuing taunts and threats as they walked away. This time there would have to be a submission or a death from exhaustion. I saw the relief on their tired grimy faces hoping for a reprieve as I walked out on the terrace to unpeg a line of washing. 'Tea will be in ten minutes' I shouted to them walking back into the house without attempting to separate them. Their safety net was gone. Although Mark was smaller and lighter than Simon he was wiry and muscular and had a streak of pure stubbornness in him that I sympathised with because I knew that, like me, you could hang draw and quarter him and he would never give in. Simon had the advantage of height and weight but he was a chubbier and while his pride was at stake he lacked resolve and belief in himself to fight to the finish. By the time tea was on the table they clattered in the back door, washed up and were ready to eat. There was no discussion on winners or losers. I had no idea who had submitted to whom.

Ann got home and joined us. 'Well what have you lot been up to' she enquired looking around the table? Children who had never bothered to comply with my directive not to speak with their mouths full decided this was a perfect time to obey, so butter wouldn't melt faces smiled enigmatically back. There was none of the usual procrastinations from the boys at bedtime; they were in bed and asleep by lights out. The outcome was that while we had no more fights, it didn't stop virtual annihilation in marathon games of Risk, or the occasional poke or shove, but their assaults were now confined to verbal insults and squabbling which involved casting aspersions on each other's legitimacy and the exchange of muttered crude Anglo- Saxon words.

Battles over the 'Risk' board game were more difficult to resolve. The primary object of Risk is "world domination," or "to occupy every territory on the board and in so doing, eliminate all other players".

Players control armies with which they attempt to capture territories from other players, with results determined by the roll of a dice. On a storm blown Saturday night in Sussex a few years hence Mark and I were the last two opponents that saw us battle scarred but still fighting for survival at 3.00am. Neither of us had a hope of supremacy, but neither of us would surrender, both hoping that a roll of the die would ease our plight. However, the fickle finger of fate, or more accurately the paw of a black panther scattered our armies and with a pounce took command of the board. We both feigned disappointment while our hearts soared with relief.

Chapter 15

Sand, Sea and Shangri-La.

The fallout from the Easter holidays was still being felt, particularly by Peter, so come the school break for the summer holidays enough money was scraped together to rent a holiday let in East Wittering for a fortnight. Not as upmarket as the West Wittering Conservation Area's sandy beach, the house, on the East's shingle beach, had the advantage of fronting on to the sea which was wonderful. The sound of waves breaking on the shingle at high tide and the screeches of the herring gulls flying down the Solent are abiding memories. The houses other great advantages were that it was detached, commodious, shabby and basically furnished so ideal for boisterous noisy children. Despite this we had to pay a deposit against damages so to encourage responsible behaviour Peter promised the children a financial reward if our deposit was returned. It was, and they duly benefited. By the time the owner discovered the loose banister newel, the broken bed leg, the tennis ball blocking the gutter and the soot covered barbeque stand we were long gone.

That summer of 1960 was a special one. It was to be the first and last holiday the family took as a family. In an era before mobile phones and no landline in the house there were no outside demands on parental attention so the children responded positively and harmony was the order of the day. While the weather held, the boys spent most of the day on the beach with Peter exploring rock pools, making spectacular sandcastles or burying him in the sand. On more miserable days, they escaped the weather with games of chess or House of Brahma building. The rest of us went off in the van investigating Saxon Churches and picking fruit and purchasing produce from local farms.

John, a sturdy thirteen-month-old was just about walking and with a weight on the 97th percentile was too heavy to carry so wherever we went we had to take a pushchair. Vanessa a much lighter burden could be carried with ease. Ann had shown me how to carry her African style on my back her weight distributed in a length of cloth. This unorthodox mode of transportation did not escape comment and strange looks from the local inhabitants.

Emma despite her bossiness and sulkiness loved playing mother so chose to carry Vanessa on her hip when she took over, a method Vanessa much preferred. I was duly appreciative of the respite because although the latter's regurgitation problems had almost ceased she was not above a spurious puke down my back.

Jane was a bit lost when it came to decision making about how she wanted to spend her time, and if chewing her fingers was taken as a sign of her agitation asking her to choose was torture for her. If she came in the van she would have preferred to stay with Peter and vica versa.

Put to the test I would say that Simon and Mark got most out of the holiday. Their opportunities for father-son bonding made such a difference to their behaviour. Our daily eating routine reinforced this bond as the three of them took responsibility for feeding us. Decades before Heston Blumenthal's eccentric food combination's we had Marks exotic lunch time sandwiches. The combinations of (1) ham and peanut butter spread, (2) cheese, onion and smarties, or (3) egg and mushroom were definitely acquired tastes however I did quite like (4) the squashed date and cucumber ones. Our evening barbeques were made sumptuous with the proceeds of our farm shop purchases. With Peter overseeing the cooking I felt I could relax my duty to keep an eye on the boys so imagine my amazement when on our last night there was an almighty whoosh as the barbeque tray was engulfed in flames. Scooping up enough sand to douse the flames we looked at our ruined dinner. Ann's wrath was monumental as she ripped into the boys who stood there looking sheepish. Not a word from either of them as they wilted under the barrage of ire. She showed no signs of running out of steam until a shamefaced voice intervened to confess

'It was my fault.'

Looking at the eyebrowless scorched penitent we waited for an explanation. The culprit had become impatient at how long the charcoal was taking to glow so had poured petrol on to hasten the process. The resultant conflagration was unexpected and I think salutary because he never went near another barbeque. His sons also developed a healthy respect for fire; however, fireworks and spontaneous combustion would be whole new ball games.

The damp hungry end to our holiday was forgotten when a few weeks later Ann announced that she was pregnant. The coming of 'Him' was not going to be the only event that would portent great changes in the household.

Chapter 16

Fossils and Tadpoles.

1961 was an eventful year that saw the start of the space race, Peter's elevation to Consultant status and, on May Day, the birth of a nine-pound dimpled bundle of joy. Apart from some initial disappointment from the girls that he was a boy everybody was soon quarrelling about who should look after him. Preselected names were abandoned and he was named Adam, or first born, despite being sixth in line. Unable to pronounce his name he was 'Him' to John and Vanessa for the first couple of years. This was in no way meant in a derogatory dismissive sense but a valiant attempt to say 'Adam'. He was an extremely good natured tolerant baby who never got the opportunity to cry even if he had the desire to do so. John, nearly two and Vanessa 15 mths were bemused but unfazed by the usurper being far too busy getting into mischief of their own making if not kept under consent surveillance. With them both on their feet it was like having demonic twins to chase. Emulating Houdini they had mastered the art of escapology so that formerly child proof playpens, safety gates, cot sides, cupboard handles and back door catch were no longer fit for purpose.

Ann had breast fed all her children for the first six weeks but Adam's insatiable appetite saw him on solids by the time he was two weeks old. Like all fads and fancies on child rearing he was born at a time when early weaning was in vogue. It was agreed that he would sleep in the small dressing room off his parent's room while Ann was breast feeding but from week one he slept through the night so there was no reason why he could not move up to baby world with Jane, John, Vanessa and me. By now the latter duo shared a room, still sleeping in cots, while Jane had a room of her own. Adam would initially share my room in a newly reconditioned cot. We were still not financially solvent enough to indulge in new baby equipment and with John and Vanessa still using what we had we would need three of everything. With the family Child Allowance now increased by ten shillings a week, Ann used it to increase Lily, Molly's and my wages by 3s.3d. Their comments should be allowed to die with them.

Although some of the joys of parenting are right up there with trepanning, life in general was reasonably peaceful and orderly. Questions and admonitions had now taken on a single word shorthand of their own, inflection being the clue to the required response from the children

Teeth? Have you brushed them?

TEETH! Go and brush them!

Kit have you put it out for washing?

KIT! Go and get it!

Homework? Have you done it?

HOMEWORK! Go and do it!

Room? Is it tidy? (As if!)

ROOM! And I don't want to see you until …

A tense summer holiday was spent at Glasses. Luckily Mark's interests had now turned to Palaeontology so off fossil hunting and flint arrowhead collecting he spent most of his time wading and sifting through a nearby stream. To encourage his and Simon's interest in stream exploring Oma promised them a small reward for any glass or pottery items they found. Glasses had been built on the site of a medieval glass making area and the Romans had in their time had settlements in West Sussex so they would not be wasting their time. During these activities, Mark, had come across a badger set which we went out to explore late one evening. The highlight of the quest was me tumbling head over heels down a slope and having to be rescued dripping wet from the stream much to the children's glee. The glittering feral eyes looking on probably had a good laugh as well.

Emma, we hardly saw. Now aged seven she was an assured and fierce pony rider expertly kicking her mount on, intent on winning every event at local gymkhanas. She was a joy to watch. Jane had progressed to riding off the lead, but had no confidence in her mischievous Therwell type Shetland mount, Tweety, complying with the gentle tap of her feet on his sides to get him to walk on. If she was presumptuous enough to repeat the tap he would respond with a sudden and unexpected bounce trying to dismount her, which did nothing for her nervousness. He also had great difficulty differentiating between signals for trot and gallop, usually bypassing the signal to trot. A pull on the rains to stop was often responded to with such alacrity that the rider was left to deal with Einstein's gravitational theory of time, space and motion.

Ann was now getting work in both the BBC and the publishing world so was a busy fulfilling commission and only appeared at weekends. Ensconced in an old bucket styled pram, the three babies and I, ambled around the lanes, played in the garden or joined the boys for a picnic down by the stream. Rules about not annoying Opa were still in force, but his unremittingly cantankerous attitude to the children, and his withering condemnation of Ann for producing another one like a wayside tinker did not endear him to any of us, so as well as the deaf ear I sometimes turned a blind eye to Opa baiting. His previous involvement in the early thirties in the setting up of the National Birth Control Council to provide contraception for married women who wanted to space or limit their families, thereby mitigating the twin evils of ill health and poverty, was considered enlightened in his days on the Bench, but any sign of being a reformer were now lost in the mists of time. With the availability of modern birth control methods on the NHS he seemed to consider Ann's continual production of children a personal affront.

Simon and Marks favourite tease was to creep up to his study and shoot small pieces of gravel from a pea shooter at the window. His bellows of rage were alarming and dramatic but his emergence through the front door was mouth dryingly terrifying. With the light behind him you could be forgiven for mistaking him for Boris Karloff in Frankenstein. There was never any evidence to find, which enraged him further, but I knew he was not above catching the criminals so persuaded them to desist. However, Emma's tease shortly before his death is still remembered.

As well as developing an interest in fossilized remains Marks collection of live creatures had still to be monitored. As long as they were in escape proof containers and were treated humanely nobody took any great exception to them until the day it started raining frogs. Not content with fossil hunting he had come across a cloud of tadpoles and unable to resist capturing them before their Froggy state had smuggled them into a dark corner of Oma's flower room, a function of the room still recorded on the servant's old bell board but then used for storing wellington boots and other wet wear apparel. I never did discover how they had been fed or if they had carnivorously devoured each other while morphing into frogs. I had opened the door to get something which allowed them their freedom, and suffice to say when they escaped into the front hall just as Claud was emerging from his study there were sufficient left to make a very impressive jumping display. This brought back childhood memories of my Aunt May in similar circumstances, and like then, I had an irrepressible urge to laugh hysterically. However, looking at Opa's murderous countenance I desisted and opened back the front door to encourage the manic frogs to be on their way. I had as much success as my young cousin Michail in days of yore. They jumped everywhere except through the wide-open front door. They were more like geckos than frogs as they stuck to walls, picture frames and jardinières. I decided to let nature take its course returning to the playroom to gather up the babies for some outdoor fun with Claud's angry roars receding in the distance.

He and I stonily ignored each other most of the time which suited me fine but I found it nerve racking when I had to take him his tea as a favour to Oma if she was out. It says something about his pernicketyness that before I took on the task I had practiced laying the tray several times before ensuring everything was in its allotted place. I heaped blessings on the head of Sr. Agatha in whose Home Economics class I had learned to make proper cucumber sandwiches. Tea was a two-step affair. I brought a tray containing a plate with four triangular cucumber or salmon paste sandwiches, two biscuits or a sliver of cake, tea pot containing hot water, empty bowl and small dish containing two thin slices of lemon and a teacup to his study on the dot of four o'clock. My lack of subservience was noticeable in my cursory knock and entrance without waiting for any acknowledgement from him. Putting the tray down I would go back to the kitchen for freshly boiled water, and on my return, I would empty hot water from tea pot into teacup to warm the cup at which time Opa heaped a measured amount of tea from his personal caddy into the prewarmed teapot to which I would add the newly boiled water. I would then empty the water from the warmed cup into the empty bowl and the bowl and I would exit the room. I'm sure he would have adored the rituals of a Japanese tea ceremony but a Geisha I was not, not even to the extent of backing out of his presence.

A servile kowtow was therefore out of the question.

Chapter 17

Departure, deceit and dispatch.

I had not been home for three years and apart from staying an occasional week end with friends had not taken a holiday since I joined the family two years previously. My Grandmothers eightieth birthday celebration was in January 1962 and although the weather was still dire everybody would be gathering in attendance.

'Two weeks' Ann exclaimed, incredulity raising her voice a couple of octaves and her eyebrows by an inch.

'You want to go home for two weeks'?

'Yes' I responded, emulating an Edwardian Skivvy standing humbly before the Lady of the House.

'What do you expect me to do for two weeks' she asked petulantly?

The obvious answer was to tell her sarcastically to stay at home for the duration looking after her own children, and putting her parenting theories to the test. Every expert knows how to raise other people's children, but when it comes to their own it's another story! However, Ann was not renowned for a sense of humour so I wasn't that foolhardy and had already persuaded Lily and Molly to do extra hours. I knew Ann would balk at this, calculating the added expense even though scrimping and saving was no longer a necessity. The day before my departure I found out her novel way of dealing with the added expenditure when she handed me my holiday wages. I had, not unreasonably, expected an additional amount of money in lieu of the board and lodgings element of my situation but when I put this to her, the response, was original to say the least.

'Your board and lodging is still here 'she told me as if stating the obvious to a halfwit.

'It's not my fault if you're not going to be here to avail yourself of it' she responded stonily to the look of disbelief on my face.

I was so outraged by her obduracy that I packed all Vanessa's and my belongs in a large second hand trunk I had acquired, and left it ready for shipping thereby ensuring I could send for it without discommoding anybody if I decided not to return. My wages had been rounded up to £4 at Christmas so I left with £8, enough for our tickets but little else. Amidst crying babies, jubilant children looking forward to two weeks of anarchy, and mixed feelings, I left to catch the evening Mail Train to Holyhead and take the night crossing to Dun Laoghaire.

Several days later I journeyed on to Galway to make arrangements with a much-loved cousin to rear Vanessa while I completed my nurse training. She tried to cajole me into leaving her there and then, but I wasn't prepared to part with her until I was ready to return to training. Vanessa has no idea how close she came to being brought up by the lovely Qualter family down a bog road. Raised with a different set of values she might have grown into a kinder, less judgemental adult. However, on return to Dublin these embryonic plans were put on hold when I found a registered letter waiting to be opened. Inside was a postal order for ten pounds, a note of apology from Ann saying how much everybody missed me and a promise that they would all be at Euston to meet me. So, it was back to West Dulwich to give it another go.

My heart sank when I saw them all at the barrier. I realised it must be half term. Jezzis wept! Were we back to square one? Scruffy, grubby, bickering kids and two snotty nosed miserable babies who cried all over me in a mixture of bewilderment, anger and relief. The latter didn't let me out of their sight for days and John's new word became 'Anme' as he followed me from room to room making sure I was not going to leave him behind again.

We were approaching the month of May and Adams first birthday before 1962 became memorable for other reasons.

Between social and work engagements Ann was seldom home before 4.00pm. Although tea time and early evening time were supposed to be set aside as 'quality time' with her children' Ann's involvement was still easily diverted by telephone calls and latterly by editing commissions. Peter was also working later so their evening meal together became less frequent. The appearance of Vesta ready meals on the evening menu became acceptable to the extent that I persuaded Ann to get a Le

Creuset cast iron slow cooking pot so that I could pre-prepare some dinners for them. With the children getting less parental time, the concerns I raised about Simon struggling in his Common Entrance classes were not so much falling on deaf ears as angry ones, his lack of gratitude and failure to live up to expectations being the theme of parental indignation. The school was intent on keeping up its reputation for the impressive percentage of its pupils who did well in the Common Entrance Exam, and the rite of passage this conferred on those going on to top Public Schools. Part of ensuring that the school maintained its high standards were the use of merit and demerit marks, the latter leading to detentions. The final step on the punishment scale was the judicious use of the cane to concentrate the minds of the twelve and thirteen year olds whose behaviour disturbed fellow pupils, or who's lack of attention goaded form teachers into giving demerits or issuing detentions. Detentions were used as a benchmark of Simon's failures instead of anybody taking the time to find out what he needed to give him a purpose to strive and develop his potential.

Only the Head was allowed to cane. Every detention was recorded in the Heads Detention Book. If three detentions were accrued in a given period of time the miscreant was summoned to the Headmasters Study for appropriate intervention, which included a caning. Simon had now reached this stage but kept everybody in ignorance by lying saying he had stayed behind in the chess club, making sure there was no tell-tale letter highlighting a third detention in his school satchel.

The following day all hell broke loose.

The Head phoned early afternoon seeking the whereabouts of 'Simon's parent's', and requesting their immediate attendance at the school. Having contacted them, Ann and Peter had gone directly there so it was Mark who came home bursting with the news that a burglar had broken into the Head's Study, vandalised his desk and stolen the Detention Book. He was also agog with the information that Simon was being interviewed by the police because he had seen it happen. Hmm...

Shortly afterwards First Born Son arrived home accompanied by parents and a police escort. I learned later when the Head announced the break-in at Assembly Simon had told his form teacher that he had seen 'the burglar' climbing through the relevant window. His description fitted Desperate Dan to a T. When he was asked by the police to show them how he had managed to see the Study from his window his first explanation for being able to see through an enormous chestnut tree in full bloom was that there had been a high wind at the time, his second was that he had been out for an early morning walk. When his room was searched, the Detention Book was found side by side with a half packet of ginger nut biscuits also purloined from the Study. Days of suspension followed with Simon brazening out his story. He never backed down from this position, initially accusing Mark of planting the goods. Peter soon put a stop to *that* with a closed study door discussion.

For me, forever associated with events of the following week is the record of Acker Bilks' 'Stranger on a shore' which was then 'Top of the Pops'. Simon spent his days mooching about in his room, listening to the radio in the playroom or amusing the 'babies,' regressing to the stage of joining them in their afternoon nap. However, by tea time, with more of an audience he was back to his usual cocky funny self, reverting to a state of total and absolute denial which reduced Emma to tears and chair kicking.

'Why doesn't he just say sorry' she would wail at me. But her concern, while entirely justifiable, was in vain. He didn't know how to appease or placate, so dealt with it by hoping it would go away.

Any wishes that Mark might have had to distance himself from the wild word of mouth stories flying around the playground were unsuccessful. The ties that bound him to his sibling were stronger. Either he was feted as the brother of a hero by pupils recorded in the Detention Book, or ended up fighting those who teased him for having a brother who was a moron.

Oma came up to London and there were a lot of huddled discussions for several days before a negotiated solution was agreed upon. School honour satisfied and family reputation intact, Simon was banished to the boarding branch of Dulwich Prep in Kent.

Chapter 18

The Martyrdom of Mrs. Grunewald.

By now there was money to spare. As well as his Consultant's salary Peter, has reluctantly set up in private practice in rooms in Harley Street with encouragement from his previous Head of Department, and with no shortage of referrals, was now earning serious money. Ann was also in demand and due to great networking skills and having cultivated the right people in her Oxford days was widening her opportunities in medical journalism. With a well-balanced bank account, she now became 'a lady who lunched' renewing old friendships and making new ones by joining the Hurlingham Tennis Club. Here, her strength, agility and sturdy build meant that she more than a match for the male members there. Unable to resist the temptation to take her on they often regretted it by the time the final score went her way. She and Peter now shared a secretary, Anne Lingham, who worked from Peters study. Ann was still working devotedly for Peter and Anne decades later. When she retired, she was well past retiring age but having initially lied on her C.V. felt she couldn't mention it when the time came. She was a good friend and a discrete secretary.

In the house, John and Vanessa got single beds and we all acquired new nylon fitted sheets to reduce Molly's ironing burden (we soon got used to the static shocks!). A delighted Lily got a floor polisher, nearly killing Peter who stepping on a previously inert rug in the hall to discover it had become a skate board on the newly waxed floor. The fact that three mesmerised babies were gazing at him in round eyed concern from the playroom doorway appeared to be lost on him as he reverted to Navy vernacular, cursing Lily into hell and out of it.

A Galt rocker supplemented the rocking horse in the playroom, an enormous climbing frame joined the see saw in the garden, and I got a Kenwood Mixer.

But the greatest change of all was going to make my life easier. I had been whinging for two years about the lack of a door between the dining room and playroom. The only access to the playroom was via the front hall which meant using a stair gate in the playroom doorway to keep the babies in if I needed to leave them to fetch something from the dining room or kitchen. My constant comment was that only a man would be stupid enough to design a house without a door to the right of the fireplace in the playroom to give access to the dining room. Now my wish was going to be granted. The work was priced up and demolition of the cupboard on the dining room side of the wall was underway when the builder discovered a lintel and evidence of a previous door. It was easily reinstated and with a step added to adjust floor height access to the playroom was achieved. There was general consensus that we didn't know how we had lived without it.

With growing prosperity, we also acquired a newish Bedford van. The poor old yellow one was ready for retirement so its green replacement got the shock of its life the first time we loaded up. Also onto the scene came Monsieur Despard a French onion and garlic seller, his seasonable ropes of produce providing an exotic smell to our basement. He was the real Mc Coy from French beret and red bandana to long sleeved striped tee shirt and baggy black trousers and turned up periodically on his well laden bike to replenish our stock. His fiery garlic breath would stop a bull. There was also Mr Kleen-Easi our door- to- door brush and polish ex-services salesman who offered us a selection of quality brushes and polishes to meet our every need. Senor (Salvo) Moretti peddling away on his treadle turning bike sharpened our knives while making flirtatious advances to Lily always threw an Italian aria in free gratis. Our blind Welsh piano tuner added our piano to his twice-yearly rounds in preparation for Mrs Grunewald and outlasted her by several years. Mrs Grunewald was a Bulgarian refugee, a widow living in straited circumstances in Crystal Palace. She was a pianist by profession and a piano teacher by trade. The latter was a thankless task particularly with her four reluctant pupils seated one after the other on the piano stool in our playroom. Four sulky children, a half hour lesson a week each, a mother who had no intention of wasting money, an expectation that I would oversee daily practice and we were in for constant battles. The poor woman tried her best. To this day, I have only to hear

Twinkle- Twinkle Little Star, Yankee Doodle Dandy and Lady of Spain to remember the weary smile on her patient face.

'Cruella de Ville' the children dubbed her but if there was any cruelty it was in their innocent carefree thoughtless childishness. Her resigned sighing admonishment of

'Rhythm, Simon',

'Intonation, Mark',

'Fingering, Emma',

'Middle C, Jane' 'find middle C' went through my heart because I knew she was flogging a barren of mules. She would probably have more success with dead donkeys. She persevered for nearly a year until the children's lack of progress wore her down. She just ceased to turn up, coinciding with Ann's resolve to curtail her services.

Every year we had a two or three day visit from a 'Gentleman of the Road' who, in return for meals and being allowed to sleep in the garage tidied up the garden. We never knew his name, only that he was from Tipperary which he pronounced as Tipper-Rary so we called him Tip. This reminded me of a girl I trained with whom we used to call 'Tip' to differentiate her from another nurse with the same surname. Our journeyman never invited conversation preferring to get on with the work he was set. He washed underneath the garden tap and did his laundry the same way. Tip carried little or nothing with him, if he drank we saw no evidence of it and what I remember most of all was his quiet dignity. His yearly arrival was anticipated but not pre-arranged, his departures silent and unobserved, the garage swept and left as he had found it apart from the odd splash of candle wax. He always reminded me of Robert Louis Stephenson's vagabond

...Or let autumn fall on me where afield I linger,
Silencing the bird on tree, biting the blue finger.
White as meal the frosty field - warm the fireside haven -
Not to autumn will I yield, not to winter even!
Let the blow fall soon or late, let what will be o'er me;
Give the face of earth around, and the road before me.

Wealth I ask not, hope nor love, nor a friend to know me;
All I ask, the heaven above and the road below me.

Chapter 19

I'm dreaming of a White Christmas.

Christmas of '62 was fast approaching and having spent a contentious free few weeks of the summer holidays at Glasses Oma had invited us for the Christmas festivities. As a ritual passed on by from her Russian-German ancestors Christmas celebrations were held on Christmas Eve. During my nurse training, I had got used to working on Christmas Day because there was an expectation that staff would put patients before their own families. This included Consultants who were expected to carve the ward turkey at mid-day on Christmas Day. This suited Peter down to the ground. Christmas Eve with the family in Sussex, drive up to London Christmas morning, carve turkey, and then home to Dulwich to an empty peaceful house. A match to the sitting room fire, a good bottle of claret, toast and Gentleman's Relish and his new Maria Callas LP. What bliss! I'm sure he hardly noticed the snow beginning to fall.

On Christmas Eve in Sussex Oma formally switched on the tree lights as soon as it got dark. Interspersed with the tree decorations were little wax candles in clip on holders. Knowing our children, I regarded this as the height of folly but Oma was a grandma who expected good behaviour and usually got it. At home, we used mismatched bargain basement delph because so much got cracked or broken, but at Oma's we all ate off a Heriot Quimper dining set and supped from a Clarice Cliff tea set. Initially I was like a hawk watching a murmuration of starlings but there were no breakages apart from me chipping the spout of a lovely teapot. We sat around in the drawing room opening presents one by one with much oohing and aahing and me keeping a note of who would need thank you letters. As in my childhood, Father Christmas came late at night to deliver one present for each child plus a stocking full of small goodies. Like my Grannie, Oma squeezed enough edibles into each stocking to ensure that none of the little piglets would require an early breakfast.

Christmas Day had forecast snow but although there was evidence of heavy frost there was no sign of it as Peter departed for London. The children were disappointed to find threatening skies and finger numbing cold temperature; however, Oma had entertaining children down to a fine art. She was a wizard at games, a connoisseur of puzzles and a gifted reader of stories. She also had an enormous trunk full of dressing up clothes where everybody could swash and buckle to their hearts content. When Adam was 9y he won a prize at the village fete as a resplendent 'Lady of Spain' complete with fan and a mantilla on his mop of hair held in place with an ivory comb. Having three babies to amuse I was grateful for her entertaining the other four. I have no recollection of Ann's contribution but I expect she had taken a reluctant Rolo, the ancient Labrador, for a walk in the nearby woods.

Rolo was one of us. His disdain for Opa was ingrained in his doggy brain. Now too old to bother barking at him he still greeted him with a show of teeth and a low wheezy growl every time he ventured into his domain, which happened to be by Oma's side where ever she happened to be sitting. Although Rolo's threat was purely reactionary it infuriated Claud. What infuriated him even more was that he could do nothing about it, at least when Rolo was alive. His thwarted revenge, when he tried to take it after Rolo went on to his kennel in the sky would have had him wagging his tail in glee.

We woke on Boxing Day to the amazing sight of several feet of snow and drifts to the height of hedgerows. Apart from the children's shrieks of delight everything else was deadly quiet. There was not a bird chirping, a hen clucking or a dog barking. We saw a Yeti coming up the drive but it turned out to be Barbara struggled up from her cottage wearing a hairy Peruvian poncho and snow shoes to inform us that not only were we snowed in but that the road to and from Graffham was impassable. As we stood discussing the implications another foot of snow, each flake the size of a sixpence, drifted down. We were supposed to be returning to London the following day but it looked unlikely, and so it proved. However, Oma, a seasoned WW2 housewife and Women's Institute Member has a larder full of jars of preserved fruits, jams, pickles, and chutneys some of which, judging by their colour and rusty lids, led me to suspect that they had stood in soldierly formation on the shelves since that era. We also had apples, pears, potatoes and onions stored in straw or wrapped individually in sheets of newspaper in a shed, a kitchen garden of winter greens currently buried beneath the snow and a chicken house full pampered lazy chickens who weren't even bothering to lay, a problem that could be remedied by a nice chicken casserole.

Oma was also prepared for outdoor fun in the snow. Her creaking attics contained a cornucopia of delights in trunks and portmanteaus buried under dust sheets. Following explicit instructions Simon and Mark emerged dusty, but triumphant with sledges, ski's, heavy duty boots and socks, Fair Isle jumpers, and outdoor clothes manufactured at a time before zips became common. With a sloping lawn, and drive, the one-man sledges and the skis were hugely enjoyed. Despite Oma's pleas to avoid a young wild cherry tree standing in shivering isolation in the middle of the lawn it endured several collisions but lived on to give us extravagant displays of spring blossom and the autumn glory of its myriad shades of red and gold leaves for years.

With everybody exhausted and ready for an early bed the elderly boiler died. There was no hope of resuscitation so the attic was raided, this time for paraffin heaters. Having found them we were baulked from using them by a lack of paraffin.

Never mind' said the ever-resourceful Oma as we kept warm by the Aga

'We'll keep the sitting room fire going and put hot water bottles in the beds'.

A search of the house for the bottles proved puzzling, but futile so we went to bed well wrapped up but without their comfort. Sometime the following day they were all back on their allotted hooks. We had had a visit from the Macking Ram. We also had a visit from the Angel of Death. Sharing a bedroom with the three babies was no great hardship and if I had not done so Adam would have died that night. Sleeping in the most ramshackle of the three cots, which they were fast outgrowing, the support holding one corner of the base of the cot gave way due to the ravages of woodworm. This tilted the mattress downwards. Adam followed, his head sliding into the gap created by the disintegrated support. Snoring noises woke me and I was about to doze off again when I realized the sounds were erratic. Getting up to investigate I found a purple faced baby slowly suffocating. Yanking him out of the gap instantly revived him but he was definitely one life short of his nine. Oma's guilt ensured that two of the woodworm infested cots were consigned to the bonfire. She invested in two stackable sorbo-rubber mattresses so sleeping arrangements became fluid depending on who was 'best friends' at bedtime.

Morning saw 'Jones the Gate', Oma's gardener and odd job man, setting too to mend the boiler while 'Long Frank' an eccentric local character versed in woodcraft and ancient lore, turned up to clear the drive. His cottage on the edge of the nearby copse was without a whiff of modern conveniences but was well garnished with maturing dead game and a cast of experienced ferrets. I never found out the origin of his name but assumed it was a joke ridiculing his skinny little nut brown frame. He was a firm favourite of Marks whose current obsession was to own and train a baby ferret. I had to admit that ferrets can make wonderful pets being playful, active, curious and loving. Their intelligence makes them interesting, and they are able to amuse themselves when you are not around. But they do require attention and interaction with their carers, and children are notoriously fickle, with attention spans much inferior to that of the dimmest ferret, so while Frank dissuaded ownership he allowed Mark to participate in their care and handling until a new obsession took hold. It was Frank who discovered the identity of the Macking Ram. Having been dispatched to the hen house to wring the neck of the plumpest laziest hen he could find he discovered Mark distributing hot water bottles in the laying spaces where the hens squatted to lay their eggs. His explanation as to his welfare reasons are forgotten in the mists of time. The frosts barely relented until March. Temperatures remained stuck below freezing point for all of January and much of February which meant that many small lakes were completely frozen over. I knew that telling children not to go on the ice was a waste of breath so I made it plain to budding Sonja Henie's or David Jenkins' that I would leave them to drown if they went through the ice and that their only hope would be Rolo.

Chapter 20

'O give me a home where desperados can roam'.

One blessing associated with the palaver involving Simon was that Claud was so busy editing his autobiography which he was about to unleash on, as it turned out, an ungrateful book buying world that he had not got wind of it. 'One Man's Furrow' was swiftly relegated to the bowels of second hand book shops, so his interest in eugenics and his theories on nature being as important as nurture in the formation of delinquency were therefore not put to the test.

Having actually read a previous book of his on the Leipzig Trials I knew he had a gift for factual and interesting report writing. His coverage of the trial of the events following the sinking of the hospital ship the Llandover was an excellent read due to his extensive knowledge of the German Language and painstaking scrutiny of Codes of Conduct enshrined in the 1906 Geneva Convention.

Every summer, before we all descended on Oma for several weeks, the older children were packed off to Forest School Camps for a week or 10 days of fun, freedom and adventure. This was Jane's first year, and at only six and a quarter, three months short of the six and a half requirement to go without an adult, an exception was made because she had three siblings going. Simon would now be a 'Trailseeker'. Mark was in the 'Woodlings' tribe, and at nine; Emma would be graduating from the 'Elves 'to join him. Bribes to stay on in the 'Elves' with Jane fell on deaf ears so Jane joined a mixed bag of children, well supervised by young adults who had joined as Elves themselves, and having gone through the 'Trackers' and 'Pathfinder' camps, were, at nineteen and twenty now enthusiastic camp leaders. The pioneers of Forest School, a progressive interwar school believed, in the need to return to a simple way of life. It was based on faith in others, do as you would be done to, and on the power of persuasion and inclusion. The individual was highly valued, but living in harmony with nature was also emphasized before Eco Warriors were ever heard of. There was no hitting, no shouting and no inconsiderate behaviour. I always hoped that some of the latter rules would rub off on our shower. When the school closed down its philosophy was transferred by mentors of the school to its offshoot, Forest School Camps. The camps were run for aeons by Ron Brand, familiarly known as Beefy. A much-loved patriarch, a legend in his lifetime, and greatly mourned in death, he left children with many happy memories.

Putting up three adults and seven growing children for any length of time at Glasses was becoming more problematic each year. Edwin, Ann's brother, now married and with a young baby (and another to follow) also had to be accommodated. However, he had a cast iron alibi for the briefness and rationing of his visits, he was allergic to horses, so although our times there seldom clashed they now had to be negotiated. With busy work schedules neither Ann nor Peter would commit to another 'holiday let' therefore a family caravan became an improbable solution. Ten people were never going to fit into a touring caravan so a large static one was considered. Whatever the size of the caravan I *knew* that Ann was unlikely to give up the comfort of her bedroom at Glasses so the caravan was going to be for me and the kids, leaving Peter the choice of sleeping under Claud's roof with Ann or joining us. Glasses tennis court was considered for the hard standing, but with the intention to refurbish it imminent the plan got nowhere. A possibility of fencing off a portion of Barbara's field was considered next but somebody on the Parish Council got wind of the plan before a Planning Application was even filled out putting a halt to any possibility of permission being granted. The only way around the problem was to buy two small touring caravans   and secrete them in Glasses grounds. There were probably more cons than pros to this solution when the nearby Wiblings Farmhouse, with two paddocks and 24 acres of woodland, came on the market.

Thanks to Oma's generosity we now had not only a holiday home but a week-end cottage and acres of space. It was across the road from Barbara's paddock and stables, 500 yards or so down the road from Glasses which was on one side of the road with the Middleheath Copse and Long Frank's house and a smattering of others on the other, and the village another half mile distant. I have long forgotten the name of the family in the pink house who owned the copse with it bridle paths and bluebell packed walk ways to which locals had unhampered access. The only downside to using it was finding Opa sitting partway along the path resting on his very own seat. On a good day, he would cordially raise his battered Panama hat to us, but usually he just glared at us as usurpers in his demesne.

The children and I were allocated Wiblings small farm house while Ann and Peter had the annex backing on to the road across a little farmyard. The single-story annex had a double bedroom, large open fired sitting room with 'a put you up sofa' and bathroom. To prevent it being turned into separate accommodation it had no kitchen. The same planning restrictions were put on the farmhouse itself several years later when we outgrew it. We could have an extension but we must have only one kitchen. The children, not used to sharing rooms, initially found the concept agreeable but quarrels about who should sleep in the top or bottom bunks soon became tedious. Luckily the big bedroom where I slept with the babies was spacious enough for four single beds until John was old enough for two of the beds to be converted back to bunk form for him and Vanessa, leaving Adam's and my single beds more space. We went to sleep to the mowing machine sounds of a nightjar carried on the still night air from a swath of deep bracken and awoke to the competition of a cuckoo and a woodpecker vying for our attention in the nearby trees.

Having embarked on caravan hunting before Wiblings went on the market Ann went ahead with a purchase of a dilapidated little green caravan which was quietly moved into a well secluded spot down our field. This became accommodation for visitors, a games room for the children when I roared at them to get out from under my feet on wet days and, in time, an enormous Wendy House for the younger ones. We got tremendous value out of it over the years despite the fact that in the long hot summer of 1965 it was abandoned to bed bugs until the Pest Control man cleared the infestation.

Chapter 21

Boys will be boys.

Those of you who have raised boys, or are raising them, will find yourself having conversations you would be unlikely to have with girls unless you have very odd daughters (but that's your problem).
You'll find yourself uttering foreign concepts like;
Put your penis away.
Beetles and ferrets are not pets.
No, you may not take the radio apart.
Yes, you may have a motorbike when you grow up
Put the seat down (as a rider to)
Who peed on the seat?
Scraping a brush across your teeth is <u>not</u> cleaning them.
Flicking a comb through your quiff is <u>not</u> combing your hair.
Necks and ears do not wash themselves.
Why are your dirty socks on the hall table?
Why does it smell of dead bodies in here?
Turning your underpants inside out does not constitute putting on clean underpants.
Wiping your bum does not require half a roll of loo paper, *or conversely*
Wiping your bum should be done with loo paper <u>not</u> the hand towel.
Washing your hands requires more than trailing your fingers through the water.
Why are door handles and switches always sticky?
Fluffy objects in pockets should not be eaten.
Chewing gum should not be swallowed or stuck on bedposts overnight.
Doing homework is not an option.
Doing homework is not negotiable.
Doing homework =20 mins. Diffusion + Diversion + Distraction =40 mins. =Hours of life you will never get back.

Chapter 22

'How much is the doggy in the window'?

I think it was about half way through 1964 before I woke up naturally. When I did so the house was eerily quiet. Silence is golden in a childless household but for those of you wise in the ways of children you will know that a silent house is just plain suspicious. I was so used to being forced into a conscious state by the demands of one or the other little fiends seeking attention that I leapt out of bed expecting to find a mad axe man had broken in and massacred everybody. Instead what I found was the *Marie Celeste*. There was no evidence of blood, but the dining room showed evidence of mayhem. There were remnants of some weird breakfast choices; tomato soup? Onion and banana sandwiches? Hmm, I wonder who?

On top of a heap of strewn pyjamas was a note in Peter's spidery doctors writing.

Back in about an hour. 'Don't worry'.

Ann had taken herself off to the Aegean for a holiday so Peter was loose with my daughter and five of his six children. 'Don't worry' seemed like the understatement of the year!

He might be a consultant psychiatrist but no sensible person would leave him in charge of six unruly children who, even the youngest age 3y knew, could not catch them to whack them if they misbehaved and who responded to his idle threats as an 'I dare you' challenge. On the first of the only three occasions he had been left to baby sit I came home to find him and two pyjama clad babies' dead to the world on the sofa in front of sitting room fire. At some point before he fell into the arms of Bacchus he had given the fire a poke and had forgotten to replace the fireguard. On the second occasion, he let the three of them loose with the hosepipe in the garden telling them to wash the ground floor windows but failed to ensure all the windows were closed. The parquet floor in the sitting room never recovered. The dent in the kitchen ceiling was a constant reminder of the day he was left to give the children lunch and failed to notice the pressure cooker valve was stuck, but he claimed that didn't count because there was nobody in the kitchen when it exploded. It took a decade for Ann to get over the trauma and allow another one into the house.

And we haven't forgotten the barbeque incident, have we?

Mid-morning six beaming children came rushing up the front steps followed by a sheepish looking Peter. In Mark's arms was a brown and white puppy. Holymuddahagod! Ann would go apeshit. No matter how many times Mark begged, her constant proclamation was 'no dogs'. This was due to some previous experience with a bad-tempered Corgi they had had to find another home for when they lived in Brixton. I could understand her reasoning, but I didn't entirely agree with her. A good natured, smart, friendly, hardy mutt would be no trouble. We had a huge garden so walks wouldn't be a problem it would just be a question of letting him out to do his business. He would have to get used to travelling at weekends but a mutt wouldn't be the end of the world. Giving this nervous looking ball of fur the once over I realized this was no mongrel from 'Battersea Dogs Home for Lost and Starving Dogs'.

'She's a pedigree King Charles Cavalier Spaniel and we got her cheap from a kennels because she was the runt of the litter' Mark informed me. I never did see her credentials but coming from farming stock 'runt of the litter' instantly raised a red flag. Her squashed face, yakky bark and bulging nervous eyes made her look at least half peke, and a more unsuitable dog for a houseful of enthuastically rowdy children would be hard to find.

'What were you thinking of?' I asked Peter accusingly as he ground coffee in the kitchen?

He tried to cajole me into connivance by giving me four good reasons why every home should a dog, none of which was relevant to our situation;

They provide companionship children (*had he counted his children lately?*)

They teach children responsibility (*ha!*)

We would be protected when he wasn't there (*lol!*)

We would be giving a stray a good home (*yeees….?*)
When I had done my Psychiatric Secondment in Brentwood in Essex they had a saying 'He's three stops beyond Barking' to identify a degree of madness.
I couldn't have agreed more. I felt like slapping him around the ears.
'Take her back and get a mutt' I advised but nobody was listening.

By the time Ann returned a few days later, the newly named Rusty, was already proving a disaster ranging from peeing nervously everywhere except outside, to regurgitating food and nipping fingers.
I don't think any of us will ever forget the day of reckoning. Ann was so ferocious with rage that I thought she would wreck the house, but apart from banging a few doors and terrifying the babies I saw and heard no more because the little ones and I decamped to feed the ducks and squirrels in Dulwich Park. I felt like saying 'It's only a dog, woman'. 'Thank your lucky stars it's not a feckin ferret or a baby muntjac deer' the latter having been top of Marks wish list since watching 'The Yearling' a few weeks before.

Rusty's reaction to the sound and the fury was to shit and puke rings around herself and to bark hysterically at Ann every time she caught a glimpse of her. However, worst was to come. Rusty was not a traveller. That was evident from her copious drooling the first Friday evening we put her in the van to go down to Wiblings. From then on, she had to be medicated toing and froing and spent the following days zonked out. The fallout from ignoring Ann's 'no dogs' edict went on for days. I was the 'how could you let them do it' culprit, while Peter had to withstand the shouts of 'what the hell were you thinking of', so innocent and guilty we both suffered. It brought back childhood memories of my Aunt May who had never met Judge Jeffrey, the hanging judge, but who had a lot in common with him. Neither of them tolerated not guilty verdicts. Aunt May's version of justice was 'you participated and / or didn't stop what was going on, ergo you were an accomplice and guilty by association.' Her 'not guilty' verdicts were zero, and this was decades before 'shared enterprise' was recognised in English law.

Ann's 'I told you so' came swiftly and repeatedly as the children quickly lost interest in Rusty whose nervous nippy reactions had not improved with familiarity. Peter got his comeuppance when, within a month of purchase he ended up with a hefty vet's bill when Rusty was diagnosed with hip dysplasia, her hip having come out of its socket for the first time. The obvious solution was to send her back from whence she came but her soulful eyes and cringing nervous demeanour had grown on us so when nobody mentioned it she stayed put by default. In time, she would leave her bed in the kitchen to sit in the playroom watching the babies. They had learned not to touch her but she was happy for them to talk to her and eventually she started wagging her tail. Soon afterwards she had to be dissuaded from begging food at mealtimes. Flat nosed breeds are not known for their brain power so she still barked indiscriminatingly at friend and foe alike. Peter now had a taste of Claud's relationship with Rolo. I think it was the clink of his leg brace that sent Rusty in paroxysms of high pitched yakking whenever she saw him. He had a Naval exchange with her one day containing dire threats and a rap with a rolled-up journal which she seemed to understand.

As well as her small brain the other obstacle to her identifying family was she had never been anywhere except the ground floor. Her dysplasiac hip did not stop her going upstairs; it was more as if she did not regard it as her territory. Constantly taking her to the top of the stairs and leaving her to find her own way down eventually paid dividends. She stopped barking at everybody apart from Molly who had a small yakky dog of her own so obviously emitted a doggy smell threat. We never did train her to a lead. I'm convinced she learned to dislocate her hip at will whenever the word 'Walkies' was uttered. The garden was her domain with the occasional trip down to the shops in the pram.

Chapter 23

Weila, Weila, Waile.

Budget airlines have now made travel to Ireland a doodle, but looking back on travelling in the sixties makes the journey look arduous instead of the adventure that it was. Five to six hours on the Irish Mail sleeper train from Euston then four to five hours on the B+I Ferry from Holyhead, arriving in Dublin Bay to a shimmering orange sea reflecting a red sunrise and the sound of church bells, squalling gulls and the clanking of metal gangplanks being secured. However, I was accompanied by three seasoned travellers age 5, 4 and 3 who were used to donning their jimjams under their clothes for the two-hour Friday evening journey down to Sussex. They would settle down to sleep on the long back seats and sleepwalk their way to bed on arrival at Wiblings. Despite the excitement of sleeping on the train and boat, and the strange noises of both, they travelled like veterans arriving set for mischief and adventure.

I was more fortunate than lots of families who couldn't afford a cabin and who had to travel seated in Lounges amongst the smell of stale porter, tobacco thickened air and schools of card playing men. To seek oxygen or respite on deck was to run the risk of being flecked by Guinness strewn vomit caught on the wind.

Remembering the upheaval surrounding my previous holiday I decided it was easier to take John and Adam with me, and to combine our departure with the oldest fours sojourn at Forest School Camps. It was no surprise when Ann gave me my wages only. What did surprise me was that apart from giving me John and Adams fare and £5 for incidental expenses there was no other funding forthcoming. However, we would be staying with my Gran so we would not go hungry. And in all honesty, I couldn't complain. On the several occasions when I had had family to stay Ann's hospitality had been unstinting and she invariably included Vanessa in any family treats, so it was swings and roundabouts.

For those of you familiar with the Artisans Dwellings you will know that we would hardly have had time to devour our breakfast of potato cakes and boiled eggs before several neighbours would have called. The grapevine was both swift and accurate so before the table was cleared all three children had disappeared down to 'The Square' behind the Dwellings to play.

'The Square' as you entered its sloped entrance from Bella Street to the left of the Dwellings had a flight of steps on the left up to the Terrace where as children we learned to walk along the balustraded wall balancing twelve foot above the Square, a strictly forbidden activity but one at which we all became proficient. The end of the Terrace had an exit to Summerhill Place and below the Terrace were the Arches where we used to scourge the elderly occupants by playing in the shelter they afforded on a wet day. Unlike the unforgiving concrete covered Square the Arches had a nice smooth tarmac floor ideal for drawing 'beds', playing hop scotch and skating. Continuing clockwise in the Square were about eight artisan cottages and then, facing the Terrace, the back entrances to the basement flats of the three blocks of our Artisan Dwellings. To complete the square was the back wall of the two cottages facing Bella Street. Thoughtfully built with no windows facing the Square it had a goal post outlined in chalk, and a bigger higher chalked outline set for games of handball. This wall was claimed by the boys, usually without contention, but sometimes the girls would make a stand and take it over for 'two ball'. Nothing much had changed from my childhood. The Square was full of playing children, the boys competing in games of handball on the back wall of the two cottages facing Bella Street, the girls, plaits and ribbons bobbing, concentrating on the intricacies of a skipping game to the words of Weila, Weila Waile. We, like them, had been children of the streets with our own game rules and rhymes, jeers and jokes, mnemonics and rites, slang and secret spells, all sucked in by osmosis to be remembered for a life time. In no time at all 'the three little foreigners 'were swallowed up only appearing at dusk to be scrubbed clean and put to bed. They were included in any games they were capable of participated in, fed, showered with sweets, and interrogated in all things that fascinate children.

They in turn were fascinated by objects in the Gran's flat. They loved looking at her 'photograph album' which was, in fact, a scrap book of memorial cards of the dead. They learned that being blessed with Holy water in the name of The Father, Son and Holy Ghost from the stoup on the wall by the front door on their way out was to protect them from harm. Magic! They also learned that statues were not dolls but likenesses of Saints who were good people to be prayed to when God was busy. They particularly liked Our Lady of Lourdes who glowed in the dark, but were completely captivated by the big picture of the Sacred Heart facing the foot of the bed with the little red lamp beneath it. As a child, I had drifted off to sleep looking at the faded rambling rose wallpaper pattern caught in its circle of light. The roses glowed red as I had listened to the murmur of Granda and Gran's voices talking about the events of the day and the 'twish twish' sounds of shoe cleaning brushes as he polished and buffed all our shoes, a ritual he performed every night.

I don't remember exactly when the Gran realised she had two heathens under her roof. I had started a bed time ritual with them of getting all three of them to recite
'Angel of God my Guardian dear
To whom God's love commits me here
Ever this night be at my side
To light and guard to rule and guide

That and their 'God Bless everybody' prayers had hidden the fact the John and Adam were not baptised. In fact, despite the older children attending school assemblies where prayers were said, none of them had been christened. I thought Gran would have a heart attack worrying about it. The idea of them ending up in Dante's First Circle of Hell was more than she could bear. A memory of my Cousin Tommy Duggan's childhood angst about Limbo made me smile. I know she sought guidance from her Confessor Monsignor O'Reilly after which she no longer voiced any concerns. I never found out if any sprinkling of water was involved. Perish the thought!

Chapter 24

Accidents, poisonings and explosions.

There are some years that are memorable for the wrong reason and 1965 was the first of several. That year we spent more than our fair of time in Accident Emergency Departments known as 'Casualty' back then. Adam started of the year tumbling down a flight of stairs and fracturing his clavicle, Vanessa used up one of her nine lives going over the handlebars of her bike landing on her face and cracking two front teeth, then a second, falling out of a tree ending up concussed and with a gashed knee, followed by cutting the pulp of a finger off. The latter I stuck back on because by then we had been in Casualty so many times we were beginning to raise 'Causes for Concern' in their little black book. I bet if we had been Council Tenants we would have by then be having visits from 'The Welfare' or the NSPPC. John had been knocked out by a cricket ball sustaining no damage but the skull x-ray showed he had several impacted stones up his nose which had obviously been there since his toddler orifice exploring period. Jane's exploits were more spectacular and memorable. She and her little friends enjoyed playing 'shop' in the garden. I used to keep, and fill, little jars for her one of which contained raisins. I was about to replenish the jar when I noticed the previously empty jar was full and they were all eating 'raisins'. When I asked Jane where they had come from she pointed to the Laburnum tree in pod. 999, six children in ambulance, Ipecacuana in Casualty, trying to explain the situation to the mothers of the two visiting children, a state of affairs I never wanted to experience again. But I did.

Three weeks later, same scenario and the same children. Having scrutinised content of all jars I got diverted before I had a chance to bring out a jug of lemonade. Jane fetches lemonade from kitchen. I go to table to pick up jug of water softener for washing machine to discover it had disappeared but that jug of lemonade is still there. Too late! Luckily it had tasted vile so not much was consumed. 999, six children packed into ambulance but no Ipecac to make them puke this time. I think they were given milk to drink. Parents not so understanding and decline further invitations to play.

For those of you who do not know what a Ginger Beer Plant is let me enlighten you. Firstly, it is not a plant but is a jelly-like sour smelling substance derived from a special type of yeast and a bacterium. The Ginger Beer produced by the GBP is real ginger beer, mildly alcoholic and Aficionados nurture a GBP as they would a generational sour dough starter and regard you as a murderer if you inadvertently kill it. If it survives it increases and multiplies and you will end up with more GBP than you started with, and this is where your problems begin – what to do with this monstrous living organism that looks to you for love and attention? Well normally you make Ginger Beer ad infinitum, and that probably would have been our fate if we hadn't been bombed.

Before going any further, I would ask you to note that in my five years in the household I had *never* heard anybody say.

'Is there any Ginger Beer in the house'?

Can you put some Ginger Beer on Buckley's order'?

'It's not f-a-i-r, why don't we ever have Ginger Beer?

I don't remember who gave Peter the GBP but he decided it would be a nice fatherly thing to do to make Ginger Beer with his offspring.

Stage one was faultless. Clean enamel bucket (used for soaking nappies in a previous life). Cooled boiled water, sugar, lemon juice, cream of tartar plus grated ginger, the latter in a piece of muslin and when sugar had dissolved the GBP was added and the bucket covered. All the children found it fascinating watching the fermentation process. The lid was more off than on as little jelly "crystals", buoyed by $C°2$ floated up and down in the bucket like frogspawn and I'm sure that over the next five days more than a few colonies of extraneous bacteria were added.

Stage two which should have been on day five had to wait for the week end so two days late the liquid was sieved and carefully funnelled into scalded swing topped bottles leaving a GBP now doubled in size like an alien Triffid. Rinsed in fresh water and wrapped in clean muslin the GBP was ready to procreate again.

At this point it seemed that only I could foresee any problems with the process. The dozen or so bottles of the fermenting brew needed to be drunk within three or four days before explosive levels of $C^{\circ}2$ were reached. 'Don't be silly' said the Homebrew Expert.

'A week will make it fizzier'. Hmm

'Let's make some more' said the Keen Apprentices.

Stored in the larder the brew fermented nicely and made a drinkable Ginger Beer, but as Euripides said 'The mills of the Gods, grind exceedingly slow, but grind exceedingly fine" and before long carelessness crept in. Labelling went by the way side and batches became unidentifiable and when I could hardly get into the larder without tripping over crates of Ginger Beer my firm ultimatum was *'no more Ginger Beer until this lot is moved down to the cellar'.*

The Lord of the Dance hearing my futile cry decided to take a hand. Mid-morning on a sunlit Saturday I was in the kitchen preparing lunch when the house was rocked by explosion after explosion. For five years, I had rained curses on the previous leaseholders for blocking access to the larder from the kitchen, creating a door from the larder into the dining room instead. Now I was heaping Blessings on their heads because the door of the larder had been blown open by the power of the blasts and half the dining room was filled with the shrapnel of broken glass and projectile tins from the larder shelves. The overriding smell was one of fermentation as Ginger Beer dripped from the walls and ceiling. The two panes of glass in the window in the larder had been blown out, those in the dining room were far enough away to escape but the curtains got a liberal shower of the brew. Initially we were all too stunned and thankful to apportion blame, but human nature being what it is it followed, and with it my Aunt Mays Judge Jeffrey type justice;

'Why did you let them store it in the larder' Ann enquired none too forgivingly?

This implied that as well as being responsible for the children's behaviour I was also responsible for her husband's. A memory of Emma's *'It's not f-a-i-r'* cry of yore came to mind when she objected to me telling her to clean her teeth but not Peter. So, as with Aunt May, there was no such thing as a Not Guilty verdict! I had visions of Jane never setting foot in the dining room again after her Bendix phobia, but at nine she was older and more resilient and it made a good story at 'Share and Tell' time at school.

Into autumn and Ginger Beer making still a vivid memory Peter decided that he and the boys would create a vegetable patch in the wilderness at the bottom of the garden.' Tips' yearly visit precipitated the plan. Since Peter was physically incapable of anything but the lightest digging Tip was engaged to uproot the wilderness. However, telling Peter that Tip was going to be doing work that required four strong limbs was like telling Mark not to keep creepy crawlies in tins, a waste of breath. Within minutes of picking up a fork he had managed to stab himself in the foot with the prongs, marking our last visit to Casualty for the year.

However, our biggest disaster of 1965 was still to come.

Hallowe'en was upon us. Our freshly decorated dining room smelled of paint, and the paste was still drying on the newly wallpapered walls. The wooden floor of the larder still exuded a smell of fermentation but apart from that it was as if the explosion had never happened. With the back garden tamed, Father of the Year decided a bonfire on Guy Fawkes would be ideal for getting rid of the uprooted jungle cleared by Tip. And of course, you can't have a bonfire without fireworks. I can only assume that when he removed the boxes of fireworks from the boot of his car late in the evening he couldn't face negotiating the cellar stairs so placed the boxes under the dining room sideboard in the hope that nobody would see them. However, he obviously underestimated the foraging skills of Son No.1 and the hawk eye scanning skills of Son No.2 who early the next morning, found, and opened, all three boxes. Wide eyed with surprise and breathless with delight they thought it would do no harm to light a few sparklers. The fatal flaw in their plan was they held them over the boxes of Rockets, Catherine Wheels and Erupting Volcanoes while they were doing so. The resultant display was probably as spectacular as Krakatau, and could have been just as deadly, but they escaped with their lives and the house still standing. Luckily it was a few years before IRA attacks started on the mainland so no riot squad arrived, just an unnecessary fire brigade whose Fire Chief tried to have a word with the Man of the House about storing fireworks. Alas all he saw of him were the rear lights of his car disappearing out the gate. The room was wrecked. Scorch marks everywhere. It was the one time I escaped without reflected blame though I did have to oversee the months grounding…of the boys that is.

Chapter 25

Infections, Inoculations and Infestations.

Siblings endlessly bicker, covet and 'borrow' possessions, tell tales and inflect pain on each other, but beneath it all there are ties that bind, and when they band together they share more than toothpaste. Siblings are very generous when it comes to sharing infections and infestations.
Coming from a family who believed in letting nature take its course, an immunisation needle never penetrated my skin until I started nursing when I was treated like Thyroid Mary by a scandalised Medical Officer. Despite the fact that Peter had nearly died when he had contacted polio Ann was very casual, as had my family been, about childhood infectious diseases. This was an era when parents held 'Infection Parties' trying to ensure their children got the disease at a convenient time. If they couldn't arrange a visit the party giver sent a lollypop well licked by the infected child to the healthy one to try to insure the disease was passed on. Suffice to say our seven never showed *any* consideration about when they became infected. For a while Jane was the most inconsiderate choosing consecutive Christmas Eves to succumb to measles and chickenpox. However, on both occasions she managed to infect John, Vanessa and Adam timing their lack of resistance to within 24 hours of each other which made life easier. Simon got mumps the morning of departure on a Forest School Camp. With an incubation period of up to 16 days Ann took the chance that Mark, Emma and Jane would be home again before they looked like hamsters, ignoring the fact that they would probably infect half the camp in the prodromal stage. Emma escaped chicken pox first time around coming down with it when staying with Barbara, she then outdid Jane becoming the most inconsiderate child in the family by passing the chickenpox varicella-zoster virus to Oma who had obviously had the remains of the inactive strain in her nerve tissue. She developed shingles from the reactivated virus and was very ill indeed.
If anybody had told me that Barbara would then top the inconsiderate list I wouldn't have given them credence, but on return from a stay in

Peru she managed it with no short measure. Classic symptoms of coughing, night sweats and weight loss went undiagnosed for months because she was in the wrong social class and ethnic group. When Tuberculosis *was* diagnosed, we were besieged by Public Health and Infectious Disease Prevention professionals. Chest X-rays, Mantoux Tests and contact tracing were as nothing compared to informing the schools, the latter being done despite all of us showing no signs of infection. As the word spread we became pariahs, influenced no doubt by our propensity for poisoning children who came to tea. One positive thing did however come out of it. Dr. Gottlieb, our long-suffering family doctor put his foot down about immunisation and jabbed everybody for diseases they had probably already enjoyed, or would only acquire paddling up the Limpopo River.

Luckily our brush with tuberculosis came some time after Ann had published an article in a medical magazine extolling the theory that a little dirt did children no harm, or conversely that we kept our children far too clean. This article gained a wide spread audience after been taken up as a news item by the BBC 'In Town Tonight' television programme. Our well-scrubbed children had to be scruffed up before the television crew arrived and we had to hope that Marks scabies would go unnoticed despite the fading Gentian Violet stains between his fingers. 'Letters to the Editor' in the Evening Standard and other newspapers were equally pro and con and the ensuing fierce debate saw more feature writers and photographers dispatched to take photographs. Even Maggie Thatcher, then a front bench member of the Government, and mother of twins, got involved. I was offered substantial remuneration by a Sunday tabloid to air my views, but declined so did not have to disclose our brief encounters with ringworm, thread worms, fleas and lice. The only infestation we had not enjoyed to date was bedbugs. They were still to come.

Chapter 26

Hoists, fibs and flights of fancy.

All kids lie and although lying is a normal part of a child's development if you want a child to value honesty it's not something that can be overlooked.

In most cases, 3- 4- or 5-year-olds are too young to understand exactly what a lie is. Their fairy-tale accounts of events are the result of an imagination working in high gear because they are still learning to differentiate between reality and fantasy, so living with children, you may sometimes feel you're in Cloud Cuckoo Land trying to determine which statements that come out of a child's mouth are real, and which are figments of their imagination. However here are some of the three little Pinocchio's no brainers…

'I didn't crayon on the wall,' said 3-year-old Adam standing by an eye level drawing with a crayon in his hand.

'I didn't leave the door open' contribution from Vanessa age 4 removing her wellies in sole command of a windblown leaf strewn hall.

'I didn't take out all these toys, Rusty did' response from John age 5 when asked to tidy playroom.

So, a year or two along, their Graffham School Fete hoist was easy to spot. Guilt was written all over their cherubic faces as they tried to hide the spoils of their 'grand theft auto'. Spread out on the caravan table was a collection of Dinky cars that would gladden the heart of any connoisseur and which common sense, divided by the amount of their combined pocket money, told me were not legitimate purchases. Admission of the robbery achieved, retribution was swift as I marched them back to the Empire Hall to confess all to the Headmistress, Miss Beevor. However, the latter course of action was thwarted when we discovered the Hall locked and everybody departed. I might have let the car jackers off with the fright of the walk to the Village to confess, but interpreting a look of smug satisfaction between John and Vanessa I knew that letting them get away with it was out of the question so marched them on to the Rectory. The Reverent Nash was an astute man who grasping the reason for disturbing the compilation of his Sunday Sermon without too much difficulty and invited the three delinquents into his study to discuss the matter. I don't know what transpired but they accepted their punishment with good grace and weeded the Village Tennis Court until it met with his satisfaction.

   Older and wiser Jane, Emma's and Marks lies were always half hearted and mostly focused on avoiding tasks in order to watch television. Recurrent themes…

'Yes, I *have* done my homework'

'Yes, I *have* unpacked my games kit

'Yes, I *have* put my bike away'

'Yes, I *am* ready for school in the morning'

But Simon's stealing, at 14, was still a cause for concern, and because he didn't like getting caught, he would often lie or stretch the truth, but would never back down and admit it. I was about to say admit his guilt but the whole point was he never appeared to feel any. Children usually lie for a variety of reasons. They sometimes feel they are not liked and believe that telling lies will make people like them more, or they distort the truth to get attention or to avoid the consequences they believe will happen if the truth emerges. The latter usually brings the kind of attention which rarely makes them feel good about themselves. Children also lie to keep their parents or teachers happy, but whatever Simons reason, the outcome was that there were no consistent consequences at home to ensure that he got the message that stealing and lying were never acceptable and would not be tolerated. For liberal parents who saw tolerance as a virtue, their indifference to his behaviour lacked any principled response

   As adults, we each have our own set of values that determine which aspects of life we regard as important. For children, parents and other caregivers are a key influence in instilling values. So, too are teachers and any religious background we experience. Having been brought up in a catholic home, and attending a convent school, obeying the ten commandments had been an integral part of my childhood so that when I had been deemed old enough to know right from wrong I was expected to go to weekly confession. This was no problem. What had a more chastising effect was the knowledge that the crucified Jesus, my Guardian Angel, my deceased mother and all the Heavenly Hosts were privy to any wrongdoing I was engaging in!

While values are liable to change as we grow and reach different stages of life the core values we learn as children remain, be kind, be truthful, and be diligent. To deny children this grounding does them no favours. Kids need boundaries, they need structure and the happiest ones live in families where there are clear rules and consequences for breaking them. In taking the road of accepting excuses for his stealing Simon's need to do so was never explored. In comparison, the consistency of the pastoral care at Cranbrook, his boarding school, seemed to work, and his steady progress, conformity and good end of term reports assured him a place at a renowned Public School.

Peter's flights of fancy with the Macking Ram and Billy (his spy) were still part of his story telling to 'The Babies' who had for some time been objecting to being called 'The Babies'. To jump ahead to a time when we went on a caravanning holiday in Co. Wicklow they had more or less accepted them as 'pretend' though still believing in Father Christmas they weren't *quite* sure. Imagine their amazement when the four of us turned up to our caravan nestled in the dunes of Brittas Bay to find Billy trying to eat a discarded tea towel on the clothes line attached to our caravan. A bigger, smellier, more annoying Billy Goat Gruff would be hard to find. He was always within sight and would devour anything left outside, shoes, tee shirts and food wrappings like an all purpose waste disposal unit.

During the holiday, there was a spectacular storm one night and I didn't dare go to bed in case the caravan turned over which it tried hard to do every time its four wheels were lifted off the ground by the gale force winds. Being down among the sand dunes saved us; caravans of families who choose the view from the headland were decimated. Needless to say, the three adventurers slept through it all and were up at sunrise to view the aftermath. As a result of the storm hundreds of dead star fish were washed up on the shore. They thought the star fish were very pretty and while I dozed off for a well-deserved nap they brought buckets full up to the caravan spreading them out in patterns on the sand. By the following day the smell of dead fish rotting in the sun was overwhelming. I waited in vain for Billy to hoover them up only to find there *was* one thing the he wouldn't eat. When we got back to Dulwich the three of them were all agog to tell Peter about their holiday to find he had already had a full report from Billy. So, belief in Billy lived on. Had I done the right thing? Hmm...

The consequences of another little fib on my part was more long lasting and puzzled the youngest three for years. Mark was by this time a weekly boarder and had out grown his wildlife phase having gone from hamsters to gerbils to little white mice, with a brief interlude with flea ridden hedgehogs and a baby squirrel with warble fly. Hamsters had been the bane of my life. One had escaped up a chimney breast and continued to live out the rest of its life there; another had disappeared altogether and reappeared when it had completely devoured the innards of a sofa. Gerbils were sweet but didn't do well, we were always holding funerals. Mark's mice thrived and happily resorted to cannibalism when they got tired of increasing and multiplying. Those that survived he sold, generously giving a male each to John, Adam and Vanessa. Unfortunately, sexing mice was not his speciality so by the time they were all packed off to Forest School Camp for their yearly anarchic holiday the large cracked fish tank the mice were in the derelict glasshouse numbered 69 and were on the cusp of another battle for the survival of the fittest.

'Sod this for a game of soldiers' said an irritated Father.

'Give me a hand to tip it up' he said grasping one side.

It took the two of us to turn the tank on its side to allow the mice to escape into the surrounding gardens. Not one of them ever reappeared so local predators must have had a field day. If the Townsend's next door suffered an invasion we heard nothing about it. We had a very fraught relationship with the Colonel re confiscated balls and apple scrumping, but his wife, Stella, and I got on well and she was quite sympathetic to returning balls and ignoring raids on their fruit trees. I would have been happy to reciprocate her tolerance had her children been as unruly as ours, but she had charming, polite, well brought up children all skilled at playing ball within the confines of their own garden, and with nothing worth scrumping in ours, there was no need for a quid pro quo

For years three puzzled children wondered how 69 mice managed to turn a fish tank on its side. Mark must have known, but he never let on. Years later I confessed and was treated as a mass murderer by my daughter, but worse, a mass murderer who told lies.

Chapter 27

Mene, Mene, Tekel u-Pharsin.

Sometime during the spring of 1967 I realised Peter was having an affair. There had been a marked lack of harmony in Ann and his relationship for about a year which had got progressively worse over the previous months. Ann's earning power increased allowing her to pursue her own interests and cultivate new friends while Peter worked later and later reluctantly being sucked in to building a private practice when he would have preferred to be engaged in clinical research. Eating an evening meal together had become a rarity except when Simon and Mark were home from boarding school because at 14 and 13 years they were considered old enough join them.   Dinner parties were few and far between and consisted of a select group of colleagues who had been their contemporaries at St. Thomas' Medical School. Peter was not so much anti-social as reserved so had to psyche himself up to entertain people, which he did with great reluctance. A glass or two of an acceptable wine and his considerable charm inevitably broke through ending on the doorstep with a 'We must do that again soon' and meaning it…until the next time.

  My suspicions about a clandestine relationship were aroused as a consequence of Peter being housebound for nearly a fortnight as a result of a neglected injury to his weak leg degenerating into an ulcer at the site of the ankle strap of his leg brace. He was supposed to be confined to bed with his leg raised but continually flouted Dr. Gottlieb's instructions, and since I hadn't been issued with a strait jacket or a badge saying 'I'm in charge' there was little I could do about it. I became an unwitting accomplice in his correspondence with the new lady in his life posting a daily letter which he stamped and asked me to take straight to the post box outside the Sorting Office a hundred yards or so up the road. Ill or not he started coming downstairs early enough to be the one to sort the first postal delivery of the day removing personal post from Ann's scrutiny. I don't know at what point Ann became aware of the situation but her unhappiness and fury was felt by all of us as they ceased sharing a bedroom. The dressing room beside their shared bedroom became his sleeping quarters while making use of Simon's room during term time. Mark, being a weekly boarder, was home at weekends but since you could never be sure what the perpetual hint of decomposition was in his bedroom the dressing room was a preferred option.

I don't know which were worse Ann's rages or her periods of icy politeness. This led me to ponder if family life as we knew it was over. The children responded to both extremes with unnervingly compliant behaviour to the extent that I longed for our morning and evening battles. Ann took up smoking again. Having been a very heavy smoker in the past she had given up cigarettes when pregnant with Jane having been hospitalised with bronchitis. She had had several lapses since then but had mostly stuck to cheroots. Now it was a pipe! However, when she started losing at tennis vanity kicked in and she gave up for good.

The only child causing concern at this point was John. At five he had transferred from the nursery classes at The Prep to the Infants Block and a year on was still struggling to read. Both Vanessa and Adam had caught up with him which highlighted the problem. The school insisted on a half hour daily reading session for homework which became torture for everybody concerned. His lack of interest and poor attention span were infuriating as he continued to misread the simplest words. I noticed he had no difficulty reading or spelling words that interested him like diplodocus, triceratops or tyrannosaurus rex but put a simple sentence in front of him and his eyes would glaze over with boredom or he would end up shedding tears of frustration. The concept of Dyslexia as a learning disorder impairing ability to recognize and understand written language was in its infancy in the sixties so it must have been at least another year before John was diagnosed. In the meantime, he was sent to the Head on several occasions for disruptive behaviour. His poor attention span was considered to be at the heart of the matter so remedial reading sessions, which he hated, and which did more harm than good, were advocated. The school would not allow him to write phonetically which stunted his ability to use his imagination or write stories. Their focus was on spelling and not on content. Fifty years on and knowing a bit more about children with Dyslexia John did not display many of the features which would now be classed as identifying markers. Yes, he was late learning to speak but this had much more to do with undiagnosed glue ear than speech formation. He had no difficulty learning the alphabet, making sentences or retrieving words. Like all children he mispronounced words but I would be hard put to remember which particular child was responsible for the following family favourites; aminal, bilk, bisgetti, effelent, porn shakes, wabbit and ban (van). Funnelling children into schools that achieve academic excellence is not suitable for all children, and definitely not suitable for a child with reading difficulties, but it is too easy to blame parents in hindsight. Schools based on the Steiner, Montessori and Forest Schools models were few and far between and as parents, on the whole, saw children as extensions of their own success they chose the prestige of the Public School cadre to bolster their own egos to the determent of some of their children who were not cut out to be high flyers.

 I don't know when Ann realised that Peter's affair was not a short time fling. She had been steaming open letters for some time before she confronted me to find out what I knew. Her fury knew no bounds when I tried to avoid giving a direct answer. I didn't want to lie but didn't want to mislead either, so I was pronounced guilty of taking sides, and I suppose by keeping quiet I had, hoping that it was a passing fancy. The following morning Ann got into a rage with John and Vanessa about some minor transgression at the breakfast table and because it was so over the top I intervened. Barbara, who had spent the night, sat at the table but was too stunned to say anything. Before any of us could draw breath, Ann fired me on the spot. Wow! 'What was *that* all about Barbara asked in amazement?

I gave her a potted version about what I knew. Barbara never used a swear word in her life, 'sugar' and 'drat' and admitting to being a bit 'miffed' being the limits of her annoyance, but her expression showed her battle not to use her non-verbal choice of an appropriate 'Holy Shit'.

'For heaven's sake, don't leave' she pleaded.

'She didn't mean it' she told me 'You can't leave the children with this mess going on, I'll talk to Mummy,'

Peter's pleas for me to stay were also focussed on providing continuity for the children saying there would be a separation but no divorce. I was torn between causing upheaval in Vanessa's life by returning to nursing, or staying with a family I had become very fond of so when Ann apologised I chose the latter and rode out the storm.

In an uneasy household and unable to make any alterations to the house because of the cost and leasehold restrictions, house hunting, to find a bigger house where Peter could have his own accommodation began. The Leasehold Act of 1967 changed the focus of the search when the 'Right to Buy' a Freehold became law and considerably increased the value of the house. Initially plans were made to renovate the basement, but with Ann's family's Accountants intervention much grander plans were made to deal with assets, and a formal separation rather than a judicious one was agreed. I'm sure Ann's legal representative would have decided that a Deeded Separation would not have been in her best interests because firstly, she and Peter could no longer share a marital roof, secondly, the court could exercise all the powers which it has to divide the matrimonial property etc. just as it would in the case of a divorce; and lastly the decree, if granted, would operate just like a divorce in terms of its effect on any Will - the spouse no longer taking any benefit unless a new Will is made specifically stating that is to be the case. Added to that would be the complications if she met somebody else and wanted to remarry.

What was to happen next would leave Peter and Ann tied financially both as professional colleagues and parents. Some years later I learned from Peter that the solicitor employed by Oma's family who drew up the papers, left him in no doubt that any refusal to agree would result in a letter to the GMC. His lover and later, lifelong companion 'The Lady Anne' was married to a member of the aristocracy and had become his patient on discovering that her husband had had an affair that had resulted in the birth of a child. With two legitimate children, comparable in age to Emma and John, and a title to consider, there would be no divorce, so discrete meetings would be the order of the day to keep the tabloids at bay and avoid scandal. Another factor was that despite the fact that we were half way through the Swinging Sixties and La Dolce Vita in the form of sex orgies at dinner parties and psychedelic drug taking, Family Court Judges could not be guaranteed to favour the mother in child custody cases. Back then there was no such thing as a 'no fault' divorce.

It took some time before Ann and I got back to our usual easy relationship but it helped that I did not take sides or indulge in gossip. House hunting around Kensington, Holland Park and Chelsea begun but finding something big enough with a garden, parking, within budget, and with an easy commute to Harley Street proved impossible. When a house *was* found, it was ideal for Ann and Peter but totally unsuitable for a close family life. The imposing Grade 2 Listed Georgian Townhouse with basement, five floors and mews flat over a garage with rear access through the Mews, was in need of complete renovation. The main residence was in Devonshire Place W1 which ran parallel to Harley Street and like the latter, and nearby streets, it housed prestigious consulting rooms containing medical and dental practitioners ranging from charlatans through quacks to experts in every speciality required by the affluent, the famous and the aristocratic. The house was big enough to provide two consulting rooms and a communal waiting room so Peter would be able to practice from home. The sale went ahead amid much grumbling from the children. Renovation was going to take three months which would give plenty of time to find new schools.

Although we had the freedom of Wiblings at weekends moving was going to be a huge wrench for the children especially Emma who had joined an Athletics' Club at Crystal Palace and had become one of their champion hurdlers. The vast, child friendly garden, the freedom to cycle around 'the block' and having friends to tea were more important to the younger ones, whom I'm trying very hard to no longer call 'the Babies', however they remained 'the Babies' as a shorthand collective noun for years.

Chapter 28

'Hello Muddah, Hello Faddah.

Letters from Montgomeryshire's 1967 Forest School Camp from John (8y) Vanessa (7y) and Adam (6y) were reminiscent of Allan Sherman's famous letter home from Camp Granada and just as alarming to the recipient of the following communications;

"Dear Bernadette

On saterday we went for a 3 day hike and I slept with Paul who spits and he spat at me. On Sunday morning when I was asleep he punched me in the nose.

Geoff pored boiling cup of tea on my leg by mis take. Will you send Vanessa and Adam and me some envelopes and stamps please.

Love from John

Ps we came back from our hike on Monday.

Pps on Thursday we are going to the sea-sid by coach."

***

"Dear Mummy

It is very very wet here and on Friday it was raining a lot and Adam was working hard in the rain because he was on kitchen duties and he did not like it but he had to do it. On wenstday John cut his head. You see he was next to the river and there was a little boy playing with some stones and he through a stone on John's head and that is how he got the cut but now he is better.

Lots of love from Vanessa

Xoxoxoxoxoxoxoxoxoxox

*Ps please send me two pears of long slacks the brown ones and the Big K ones. And please will you send Adam two pears of slacks. THANK YOU."***

"Dear Bernadette

Please come and take me home I hate it here everybody is horrible.

I no you will come.

Love Adam x x x

Ps I have lost my stamps"

***

"Dear Mummy

I have made lots of friends that are very nice and there names are Margaret, Jean and Bob. Bob is our leader and he is very nice. Angela and Adam sleep with me now. When Adam came here he slept with Tim and he liked it. But the next night he was a bit sad so he slept with me. Angela did not have a tent so she slept with Ben for three nights then she slept with Tim for two nights and now she sleeps with me and so does Adam. Please will you send me some more stamps and envelopes and HURRY. Adam said for me to write THIS. He did it. He saw Angela's friend. He is a man. He saw him do the loo (drawing of man peeing) and then he thought it was so funny that the man saw him and Adam ran away as fast as he could.

Lots of love Vanessa

Ps please send me two felt pens and a notebook to give Angela for her birthday."

***

"Dear Bernadette

Beefy said you could come and take me home if I want to go but I think I will stay. I am sleeping in Nessa's tent.

Thank you for sending me my trousers all my close are wet.

Love Adam x x x

***

"Dear Mimi, Peter and Billy

I am having a lovely time at camp. On wensday I climbed a very very big hill and on the way I got stuk. But Mary and Ken the people who looked after the elfs helped me and I was all right again and the sheep were very very sweet.

Lots of love from Vanessa".

***

Their stories about the enjoyment of cooking over open fires, eating while sitting on logs drawn up in a great circle, and living and playing communally flowed enthusiastically out of three damp, wood smoke smelling adventurers on their return home. Memories of kitchen duties in the rain, washing in cold water, and filling in latrines receded as they enthused about the night games, when they were woken up at 1am and taken to a location in a gully or wood to stalk each other silently through the dark country. Then there were the skills they needed to light a fire of wet wood with a single match, and cooking baked beans or bacon and runny eggs, and being taken to a bivouac site and be expected to work as a group to orientate their way back to the main camp. Also, there was the evening camp fire rally with everybody from the oldest to the youngest sitting within their 'tribes' in the circle of logs reporting back on events of the day, making music, singing songs and drinking cocoa.

Each camp had its quota of deprived children who were welcomed as participants, the only thing distinguishing them being that they arrived unequipped so had to share tents with the more fortunate children there. All children were encouraged to take a Swiss Army Knife and were quickly taught to respect its use and to take responsibility for looking after it. From long experience, I had learned that the wilder children were not given this lecture early enough so every year when drying our tents in the garden Mark and I would examine them for stab wounds. We were never disappointed.

The great sense of independence, self-reliance and social skills children gained at Forest School Camps cannot be underestimated. By the time our Babies were 8y they were travelling unaccompanied across London and had learned never to tell me they were bored. I didn't have a range for them to black-lead, or a kitchen floor to red raddle, as my Gran had, but I could still find chores for idle hands and minds.

Like Simon, Mark, Emma and Jane all three of them could be guaranteed to return from camp with one item in their rucksacks allowed to sink to the bottom, and left unopened. I never had to wonder why they returned with yellow teeth. Pepsodent never has a chance to work its magic.

Chapter 29

Upstairs, Downstairs.

The three months' renovation over-ran to the extent that we became homeless as the sale of the Dulwich house went through and late August found four Pickford Vans lined up in the drive to move us to what was still a building site, and amidst the curses of Paddy O'Leary the Project Manager, and prima donna dramatics from Vera our Viennese architect, we moved in. What should have been a chaotic fiasco was run by the Pickford's gaffer with military precision. Having overseen the packing and labelling and done a recce of our new home beforehand he lined the children up in the hall in Dulwich and with a designated mover made them responsible for seeing all their boxes ended up in their new bedrooms. With me he made sure that the first thing to be unpacked was tea making paraphernalia. He also presented me with a box which had lost its destination tag.

'Where do you want me to put this' he enquired (determined to find a home for everything)?

My heart sank when I saw it was the 'Sock Bag' from which I had removed the tag and left behind for the bin men. For six years, I had been depositing odd socks in this drawstring bag and had ended up with 49 socks, none of which made a pair. Having decided that the mystery of the missing socks would never be solved I resolved to abandon the quest and get rid of the Albatross, but there was the bloody thing back to haunt me in the hands of an obsessive-compulsive Gaffer. I had a feeling that telling him to 'lose' it would send him into a panic attack so I put it in a dark corner in the utility room where the contents, in time, increased and multiplied. Three hours later, everything in place and nothing broken our movers departed as quietly as Father Christmas. I never did get the opportunity to ask them if they had found any dead bodies in Marks room.

My first priority was togging four children out in new school uniform. John Lewis School Uniform Department wouldn't forget *us* in a hurry! Making sure everybody knew how to get to and from their new schools was the next objective. Emma at 14y had no trouble getting to and from St. Paul's in Hammersmith, Jane 12y was nervously contemplating transferring to Francis Holland in Clarence Gate the far side of Regents Park, John 9y had the most difficult journey out to The Gatehouse in Sewardstone Road in East London and I would accompany him until he was confident he could do it alone. Vanessa's school, St. Vincent's, was within walking distance. 7y old Adam had to travel across to The Hall in Hampstead but was much more worried about having to wear a pink blazer and pink school cap than the journey. Ann would drive him there in the mornings and he would come home by taxi. Eventually with highlighted underground maps and orientating skills learned at FSC they were travelling alone. If that sounds horrifying, factor in a different time and a different world. No mobile phones just their details in their breast pockets, duplicates in their satchels and instructions to travel in the carriage with the guard.

I concentrated on making O'Leary's life hell on earth until he was ready to move mountains to get out from under my feet. Within a week he only had the basement to finish and the snagging to do before Tim, the Post Office Telecommunications engineer, with reels of multi-coloured wiring, came in to connect phones throughout the house. The main Practice line was in the hall, switched through to a couple of out of hour's extension lines in Peter's Consulting room and the kitchen. The family phone's main line was in the kitchen with extensions in the hall and basement. I explain this system in some detail because of the subsequent fire!

Finding a cleaner was the next priority. Lily having taken one look at the house had decided to retire. Molly had done so earlier in the year and had been replaced by 'Mrs E', a Peggy Mount type Sergeant Major whom the children treated with the kind of respect I envied. Unlike Molly, Liz Embury has no objections to be regarded as a char, enveloping herself in a size 24 floral wrap around apron despite the fact that she was not engaged in 'rough' work. I expected her to do a Lily because she was already drawing her old age pension, but she was full of enthusiasm at the idea of working in such a grand house and went into raptures about the marble fireplaces and ornate plaster mouldings bemoaning the fact that the old names for the reception rooms on the ground and first floor would be lost to the functionality of Waiting Room and Consulting Rooms tho' the drawing room somehow hung on to its old name.

She shrewdly calculated that it would take five hours a day to clean the house.

'Too much for one person' she told me firmly.

'She'll start flagging and cutting corners and before you know it you'll be sacking her' she said nodding her head that contained decades of experience.

'Get two and that way if one lets you down you have the other to get the essentials done'.

I knew that Ann had no interest in the nitty gritty of employing cleaners. All she wanted to know was that they would be in place by the end of September and that it wasn't going to cost an arm and a leg, so over a cup of tea Mrs E and I sat down and calculated that one cleaner would need to work between 7.00-9.00am and cover the Practice area and the second cleaner would preferably work from 9.00-12.00, cover family accommodation and ideally would be able to start at 8.00am if cleaner No.1 was off sick. I knew the latter was unrealistic since most cleaners would have some family commitments.

'I'll be back first thing in the morning' she told me, failing to mention that this meant the crack of dawn. Her plan was to accost cleaners as they arrived at neighbouring Practices both to find out what the going rate was, and to seek advice about attracting applicants.

'Don't waste your money on the Evening Standard ad' she said scrunching up my carefully worded nearly completed advertisement at 10d a word.

'Word of mouth is what we need' she said handing me a notice about a lost cat taken from a nearby lamppost, sucking her hot tea from her saucer as she gauged my expression. Jezzis! I could just imagine Ann's reaction! But it wasn't going to cost her any money and if it didn't succeed she needn't know anything about it. Hmm…

A vision of Sr. Josephine and Race Day at St. Anne's flashed through my mind. My only consolation was that Ann did not have Sr. Josephine's detecting expertise or forensic cross examination skills.

At a time of limited access to zeroxing machines I press ganged the terrible trio into making A4 notices using carbon paper. I promised as many chips for tea as they could eat (yes I was now the proud possessor of a chip pan) so they added illustrations free gratis. As soon as it was dark I slipped out and sellotaped the 'Cleaners Wanted' announcements up beside the 'Lost Cat' notices.

The following morning a wiry little woman pushing 50y stood on the doorstep demanding to see 'the Madame'. O'Leary, with a leer on his face that I longed to remove surgically, came and found me having discovered the hard way that disturbing Ann, unless it was a matter of life or death, or you were carrying 'en carafe' of coffee, was not to be embarked on lightly.

'I am Amelia' she said handing me all the notices I had put up the evening before.

'I will be your new cleaner' she told me using the Imperative Tense. I assumed that this was because she was foreign and that this was an expression of interest and not a statement of intent.

`Eu sou Portuguese, I work hard, I have good references and you will pay me £5 an hour' she told me brooking no discussion.

The mention of £5 an hour really floored me since I was then earning £6.50 a week. I took her upstairs to meet Mrs E who was doing the ironing and left her to the interrogation while I made us something to drink. Liz, who had run a NAFFI during the war, knew how to deal with people, whereas I had grown up in a much more courteous society where one went around the houses before extracting personal information. I had been taught that the rituals and traditions of hospitality was to exhaust every subject under the sun until one got to the heart of the matter by circumlocution to garner the information you wanted. I believe that on this occasion Mrs E truly met her match. Amelia had demanded to see what equipment we had available and what cleaning materials would be provided, and being satisfied by our

Mr. Kleen-Easi selection was prepared to agree hours and terms. At this point I mentioned that the post would be split between two cleaners.

'That is hokaye' she told me taking out her diary.

'I can spare you two hours between 7.00 and 9.00am or between 5.00 and 7.00pm' she told me scrutinizing her timetable,

'But do not worry, my niece Elizabeta will work from 9.00 until mid day'

'She is a good girl, a good worker, de confiança,' she said as if her personal recommendation was worth a solid gold seal of approval.

This was getting out of hand. 'O que ao falar "o Doctora" e nós do terá do `I de O teve que ter referências antes que você poderia ser considerado para o emprego' I explained in my best pigeon Linguaphone Portuguese, but before I could even get the words out her hand was in her bag extracting a sheaf of glowing references including one from her Parish Priest reporting that she attended Mass and went to confession every week. I wasn't sure if the latter denoted a habitual sinner or inordinate piety.

'You will give us both a trial for one week and if you are not happy we will go, hokaye' she said, holding out her hand and standing up. Mrs E nodded agreement but I thought I should run it past Ann just in case she turned out to be a serial killer. Armed with a cup of coffee I made for her office, explained the situation and asked if she'd like to interview her. When I saw her eyes glazing over, I knew the latter was a no no.

'Take up some references but tell her I won't pay £5 an hour, that's exorbitant' she told me disappearing behind a Guardian supplement, adding 'Find out what the going rate is and if she turns out to be worth it we'll pay it'. By the end of the week's trial she was going to have to eat those words.

Amelia turned out to be wonder woman. She was like a spinning Dervish arriving on the dot of 7.00am and getting through the work without stopping for a break before going on to her next job across the street. Elizabeta, who started at 9.00, was not endowed with the same energy but likewise her work couldn't be criticized so at the end of the week's trial and faultless references I left it to Ann to engage them. In the meantime, I had found out that the going hourly rate locally for cleaners was £4.50. Although Ann now behaved as if I had no right to know what agreement they had come too I knew Amelia has stuck it out for the £5. She knew her worth which was more than Anne Lingham or I did. Neither of us had had ever had a rise commensurate with the rise in the cost of living and I knew that Mrs E's £3.50 an hour was also unlikely to rise but I made up for it by giving her lunch on the two days she came and getting Anne Lingham to pay her bus fare out of practice petty cash. By the end of September, we were down to the snagging and Pat O'Leary moved out of his makeshift office in the basement and into the Mews flat to begin the renovation there. Until that was completed Peter would share the basement with me and Adam, and Simon when he was home.

The basement could be used as separate accommodation with its own front door but we used the internal stairs to bring us up to the ground floor hall. Where once there had been a kitchen, scullery and servant's offices there were three bedrooms and my bedsitting room, a bathroom and enormous playroom with galley kitchen and eating area. Remnants of the past included a wine store and a walk in safe (don't go there!). Much to the children's delight Peter had Lilywhite's install a full-size table-tennis table to help atone for the loss of a garden. The floor of the entire basement was tiled in white thermal tiles to reflect light but they became the bane of Elizabet's life as they showed up every scuff mark from rubber soled shoes. Scrubbing with a Brillo soap pad was the only thing that got rid of them so I added the chore to my list of appropriate punishments for bad behaviour.

The ground floor was very impressive the front reception room becoming the patient's waiting room which would be shared with the Physician, Dr. King, who would rent out the adjoining Consulting room, formerly the dining room. His secretary occupied a small office next to the Cloakroom and back door where the dumb waiter from the basement kitchen had ascended. Anne Lingam didn't fare so well. Her desk was in the hallway near the bottom of the stairs with a draft from the front door every time it opened. There would have been more comfort if she could have closed the internal folding doors but the waiting room door was on the wrong side of the doors so the most she could do was unfold part of the door enough to shield her desk but not impede her view of either the front or the waiting room doors.

The first floor's vast drawing room, formerly used for gatherings on a grand scale, its three 21 paned balconied windows overlooking the street was Ann's sitting and entertaining room. In time, with a judicious rearranging of furniture, a portion of it became her Consulting Room. Peter practiced from the smaller, quieter back room once the library cum manly study of the master of the house.

Up another flight of the grand staircase was a soundproof, security, fire door behind which was the three floors of family accommodation. The second floor contained the kitchen, dining room, children's sitting cum dining room and a bathroom made from a mezzanine space stolen from where the grand staircase ended.

The next floor contained a small spare bedroom over the kitchen, Ann's bureau cum bibliothèque over the dining room, her en suite bedroom over the children's sitting/dining room, and a laundry/utility room over the bathroom. I was now reduced to one Dutch Airer in the laundry room so had to get used to the constant hum from the tumble drier. Between it, the washing machine, the fan extractor, waste disposal unit and washing up machine the luxury of a silent house while the children were at school was a thing of the past.

Lastly the top floor with five custom built study bedrooms housing Mark, Emma, Jane, John and Vanessa. The children had all chosen their own bedrooms which is how Adam and Simon had ended up in the basement with me. The floor was completed with a bathroom and a fire escape across the roof whose viability we were to test in time.

Noise and sliding down the irresistible banister to the ground floor became a daily battle ground, but since I had the excuse that I could not be responsible for behaviour I could neither see nor hear I took vicarious delight in letting Ann or Peter deal with it as a punishment for moving. However, when they passed the onerous task on to Anne Lingham I felt obliged to take it back.

Rusty became a nervous wreck. Her bed was now in the children's sitting room so we had to remember to take her down to the courtyard garden to pee. Between her and her relieving herself were the security door and two flights of stairs and *strangers* in the form of patients. Her one of two reactions was either hysterical barking or cringing terror, the latter sending her scuttling back up the stairs again where her progress was impeded by the self-closing security door. To give her due she had excellent bladder control.

Chapter 30

Archibald the Magnificent.

Archibald a sleek young black cat literally walked in through the front door one drizzling evening as I was putting out the milk bottles. He made no effort to ingratiate himself. Sitting like a sphinx he regarded me with, what was to become, a familiar inscrutable gaze. I found myself talking to him like a sentient being

'You don't live here Pussy Cat' I told him.

'Obviously not, you intellectually deficient cretin' said his supercilious glance.

'Are you the lost Pussy Cat' I enquired?

'Not any more' he indicated, walking towards John coming down the stairs.

'I like you' he told John accepting a stroke, but making no pathetic winding or meowing noises to indicate subservience.

'Canwekeephim, canwekeephim, oh, please canwekeephim? The beseeching mynah bird repetition reverberated around the hall as the mini panther calmly licked himself dry.

'He's probably the 'Missing cat' I told the Mynah Bird, 'keep him here until I find out where he lives'.

Going out in the rain I looked on every lamp post, basement railing and parking meter in the street; no longer any notices for missing cats.

Returned to an empty hall to find a besotted Mynah Bird had taken the cat upstairs and I now had to face a Greek drama chorus of canwekeephim, canwekeephim, oh p-l-e-a-s-e canwekeephim, with only one dissenting growl. The latter was soon silenced by an eyeball to eyeball confrontation with growler returning to her bed in humble defeat.

Ann was introduced and impressed, but said we could only keep him until we found his owner and that if he as much as pulled a thread in our newly covered brocaded furniture he was going to be a very dead pussy cat. The following morning, I decorated the lamp posts with CAT FOUND notices. These mysteriously disappeared. Hmm...

Anne Lingham then reluctantly carboned a note for me to put through neighbour's letterboxes, but most importantly our guest could take his leave at any time. He didn't. After several days, I knew I had to accept defeat.

'You *did* say he could stay until you found out where he lived' said the Mynah Bird, turning into a Little Elephant.

'He needs a name said the Sire of Little Elephant observing the listening cat.

He had been reading Archie and Mehitabel with him to try to get him interested in reading for pleasure so thought Mehitabel was a splendid name for a cat. I had to remind him that Mehitabel was female, and an Alley Cat, two facts that might cause offence to our young Prince.

'OK, let's call him Archie' John suggested resulting in a disdainful glance from the Prince.

'Archibald sounds grander 'proffered Mark to be greeted with the veiled eyes of one who had been sitting listening to the story of the Alley Cat and the Cockroach.

'These scuds want to name me after a Cockroach' he told Rusty as he walked off in disgust.

But Archibald he became and soon we wondered how we had lived without him.

His time table was circumscribed by daily events. He slept in the basement with Adam and had a litter tray by the basement door and a feeding station in the playroom. Every morning Adam awoke to find two mesmeric eyes sending out food signals reminding me of Jane when I first arrived. He then followed Adam and me upstairs to a communal breakfast and to say good morning to everybody. The ring of the doorbell alerted him to the arrival of the first patient of the day so descending the stairs at a regal pace he then took up his duties in the Waiting Room. Patients sat there in zombielike depressive trances, high as kites in the raptures of mania, or dizzy from self-imposed starvation, or in the case of our Physician tenant's patients, seeking a diagnosis or awaiting results.

One and all they seemed to appreciate Archibald's companionship. Being a large room chairs were placed to give patients a comfortable amount of personal space. Archibald took up residence on the two-seater sofa and gazed speculatively around encouraging any patient to rehearse their problems before they ascended the stairs to Peter or were called into Dr. King's adjoining consulting room. While he was happy to accept an occasional stroke, he was not a lap cat or a purry-purry cat so you had to accept him on his terms. He would give you his full attention if you wanted to talk, but if you just wanted his Zen like composure as you flicked through a selection of 'Country Life', 'Horse and Hound' or the Daily Telegraph that was ok. And if you wanted to just gaze into the abyss he was prepared to keep guard over you.

'That mog could keep us all in caviar if we billed the patients for his time 'said Anne Lingham half seriously.

Tea time he joined the children and had his evening meal in the kitchen. Although Archibald thought of himself as suave and sophisticated he would watch television with them or perfect his pouncing technique by chasing twitching objects on a piece of string, or if any of them wanted to concentrate on their homework he escorted them to their study bedrooms to distract them by stretching himself out on any open page needed to complete an assignment. Later, depending on whether he wanted to listen to classical music, or help Peter, he would join Ann for a gin and tonic and Mahler, or he would stretch out on Peter's desk listening to him dictating notes on the day's patients, looking for all the world as if they were conferring on diagnoses. Evenings he would watch a game of table tennis, or prevent you playing a game if he felt mischievous, batting any fallen balls across the floor like a manic squash player, then he headed for Adams bedroom ready to curl up to sleep. Occasionally, if he was bored, my sofa was honoured by a brief visit but I felt I came a long way down his priorities.

Archibald turned out to be a great traveller. On his first week-end it was decided to take him to Wiblings. Not having a cat basket, and not wanting a cat loose in the van, Ann suggested we put him in a ventilated cardboard wine box. He had shredded it before we had even started the engine; however, he was sitting calmly on Mark's lap so we closed the windows and hoping for the best we set off. He was amazing. Initially he gazed out the window with great interest but soon found a spot between a sleeping Adam and John and slept the journey away. The country side was a revelation to our inner-city Pussy. The first weekend we hardly saw him and feared he had either got lost or run way, but Sunday evening as we packed the van he was sitting on the back seat ready to go. As he got older and bolder we had to set off looking for him when we were ready to depart and one fateful week he couldn't be found. Barbara assured us she would keep an eye out for him and leave him food but she had to report that she had seen neither hide nor hair of him. We went down prepared to spend the weekend looking for his mangled body. Imagine our delight when Ann opened the door of the Annex to find an irate and very hungry Archibald ensconced. We expected to find he had toileted everywhere but he had been very civilized using the bath as a litter tray. He had used toilet water to drink but had been without food so was ravenous.

Although well settled with us we half anticipated a ring on the bell to find the previous owner had come to reclaim him so no official decision was made to adopt him. His adopting us became a fait accompli but in doing so he had to endure the mutilation of castration, the indignity of a red collar with a bell to give Sussex birds a fighting chance and an engraved medallion with his personal details. We had no notion of just how important he was to everybody until he tangled with a hungry fox on a misty November dawn patrol around Wiblings. We had heard the tussle but didn't realise for a couple of days that he has sustained an injury until he started limping. On examination Ann found four incisor marks had punctured a front leg which was showing signs of infection despite constant licking.

'He's been bitten by a fox and has osteomyelitis' said the Kentish Town vet to Ann and the vanload of children who insisted on going with her.

'He'll probably have to lose the leg' he told them (far too cheerfully in Ann's opinion)

'It's going to be expensive whatever we do, so we will have to consider the alternative' he said in code.

I don't know if she ever considered that option, or could have lived with the consequences, but after 48 hours of intravenous antibiotics Archibald was discharge back to our care, with all four legs, and a truly massive veterinary bill, and Anne Lingham could get back to her normal work load instead of having to give regular bulletins to his fan club. His greatest adventure of all occurred several years later when travelling back to London with a member of the family, who had just learned to drive. Stopping the car to have a pee in a coppice on a rural road he did not notice that Archibald had also got out for a pit stop and drove off without him. *His life was made unbearable.* He had to set out daily to search for him, leaving food as an enticement for him to stay in the area. Several days later he was rewarded finding Archibald at the spot where he had jumped out of the car. Apart from an exchange of baleful looks nothing was said. The Prince curled up on the back-seat shelf for a well-earned snooze.

Chapter 31

Mini vans and drunken nights.

Settling in to W1 and new schools took some time. The loss of the garden and a household divided by two floors were the hardest to get used to. The former was somewhat mitigated by having the key to the nearby Portland Square private garden but we only used it for after school picnics because the sight of children running around enjoying themselves sent the other desiccated users into fits of pique. We more often headed for the open space of Regents Park nearby but with the freedom of Wiblings at weekends the loss of the West Dulwich garden receded to be replaced by fierce games of table tennis in the basement playroom. Neither John nor Adam inherited Simons and Mark's competitive genes, they didn't need to, they had Vanessa to contend with. Ann took them to Seymour Hall Baths for weekly swimming lessons and I sowed the badges proclaiming their prowess and progress onto their swim suits. There was also Forest School camps to look forward to and our mega adventure of the year, a fortnight's holiday in the West of Ireland. Looking back, I can't believe that the four of us crossed England and Ireland in the back of a minivan which also contained six suitcases full of wet weather apparel because as the locals were wont to say 'Ye don't come to Connemara for the weather'.

The trio were normally great travellers but with a day, a night, and half the second day in a van, with restricted views of the passing country side, most games of the 'I Spy' genre were abandoned and there were only so many games of Racing Demon and Happy Families I could concentrate on. So, when the 'Are we nearly there yet' and 'How much further is it' enquiries began to proliferate, interspersed and punctuated with 'I feel sick' and 'I want to pee' declarations Vanessa's Uncle Sam, our driver, took over. God love him, but he felt it discourteous not to give children an answer. With at least one enquiry a mile he fed them accurate information and answered calls of nature tho' his jaw and hands were locked with tension. His wife Christine, in the passenger seat, gazed calmly ahead blissed out on a heavy-duty dose of Valium and Jelly Babies. Oh, how I envied her. Now a much-respected South African Ambassador I wonder if Uncle Sam remembers this holiday?

Actually, the holiday itself was great fun. We had rented a house in Ard na Mara in Salthill, the seaside town in Galway. Ard na Mara means Hill by the Sea so we had a view down to the sea and the long promenade. The house, like our holiday let in East Wittering was big and shabby, the only difference being that this one belonged to a Good Catholic Family. Much to the children's delight it was decorated with Holy Pictures and a selection of statues in every room. Thanks to my Gran the heathen had an impressive knowledge of the names of the Saintly ones and knew who to pray to for special favours. Uncle Sam, a Muslim, and Christine an avowed atheist, were not so impressed so removed all signs of devotion in their bedroom to the top of the wardrobe.

Walking down the hill we crossed the road opposite the Galway Bay Hotel to Ladies Beach and its spectacular views across the Bay. Its sandy beach and shallow water were safe for paddling but having learned to swim our water sprites preferred to walk further down the beach to Blackrock where there was a pier with several diving platforms at different levels. The top level is not for the faint hearted but John was not to be outdone by local kids. We spent hours watching them taking the plunge getting colder and bluer with each dive. Teeth chattering, they were revived with hot soup and would continue until the rain came, or until they were the only ones left. They pissed the Life Guard off no end because as long as they were diving he had to sit on his high chair rather than in the comfort of his hut.

As a change from Salthill we spent a day further up the coast at Spiddal to explore the rock pools before the tide came in. Sam and I get engrossed in talking but waved back politely to Christine and the dancing, gesturing children on the beach. It was only when a fellow holiday maker came wading out to shout at us that we realized the tide had come in behind us and that we would now have to negotiate chest high water to get back on the Strand. I should mention that neither of

123

us could swim though I could do a dead man's float. This was not going to be enough in this situation but might well describe its outcome.

We also went on a 'Mystery Tour' with Córas Iompair Éireann ending up at the Cliffs of Moher. Having an unknown destination meant that nobody except the driver could answer the question 'Are we there yet'? Adam developed a passion for 'Mystery Tours' on that visit and a couple of years later returned to exhaust the repertory of the local coaches. However, the highlight of the holiday for the Minors was being allowed into the local pubs for an evening's entertainment. Awash with Tizer and Finches fizzy orange and subjected to deafening music from featured folk groups, they sat through a medley of Republican and rebel songs, and their all-time favourite 'Seven Drunken Nights'. For the last song of the evening the more boisterous in the audience removed their shoes to beat time on the tables to 'The Holy Ground' or 'A Nation Once Again'. It took several sessions before I cottoned on to the fact that the Minors euphoria was not entirely due to the music and camaraderie they were enjoying, they were also surreptitiously supping the dregs of pint glasses on the tables around them.

We hadn't had a visit from Billy tho' we did see him tethered, brooding and chewing, among the furze in a field near Claregalway when we visited the Friary Graveyard to say hello to a lot of dead people I had known and loved. I had killed the Parish Priest here twenty years before. Peter therefore had a modified Report leaving out the near drowning, underage imbibing and death of the Canon. On our return to London I had a phone call from a perturbed house renter reporting that all her Holy Pictures and statues in the back-double bedroom were missing. Raining silent curses on Sam and Christine's heads I told her she would find them all on top of the wardrobe. To save the poor woman the bother of having the house blessed the words Muslim and Atheist never crossed my lips. I said they were Methodists which seemed to satisfy her.

Chapter 32

The Age of Aquarius.

The 1960's was a decade when views about psychiatric treatment tended to be polarized between psychotherapy, and physical treatments which included the use of chlorpromazine, insulin and electroconvulsive therapy. Peter's previous Head of Department was the chief proponent of the latter approach but Peter's own views about treatment evolved gradually along broader lines and he became an expert in the use of psychotropic drugs and psychotherapy'. However, psychotherapy being an unregulated field anybody could set up as a therapist and there was nothing the Health Professionals Regulation Council could do about it. It didn't help that Psychotherapy had been torn apart by factions and schisms, since the split between Freud and Jung. An umbrella body, the UK Council of Psychotherapy, was established to promote self-regulation but it splintered and was challenged by a rival organization the British Psychoanalytic Council. The regulators' difficulty is that they were attempting to police private conversations between two people which were freely entered into and which happened behind closed doors. There is still no effective regulation or licensing. Some professionals think the Councils are foolish even to try, therapy, being more of an art than a science.

Ann, seeing a niche in the possibility of referrals from Peter, who had neither the time nor inclination to take on long term behaviour therapy decided to set up in practice. Having no professional qualifications in the field she at least had enough sense to sign up for two years of psychoanalysis. Three mornings a week found her dredging up childhood memories and dismantling dreams on a nearby Psychoanalysts couch. My dreams were a great disappointment to her when she used me as a guinea pig, but my relationship with my father evoked much dissection and comparison with herself and Claud. In no time at all we had patients with more money than sense gracing the drawing room one corner of which had now become her consulting room. A new part time book keeper, Diana Tomlins, was employed to formalise the practice accounts. As Ann built up a practice a specialist field in drug related problems became her forte and her downfall.

By 1968 the world was dealing with outcries about the Vietnam War, Free Love, Flower Power, Marijuana and Beatle Mania. The Age of Aquarius was upon us. In our house, we were dealing with three Aliens now age 17y, 16y, and 14y.

Alien the Elder, the heir apparent, was doing well at Chichester but stealing was still a problem, particularly his pilfering of Peter's stock of wine. Peter was well aware of the depletion of his cellar but seemed content to ignore it. 'As long as he keeps away from the vintage stuff let it be' was his response when I raised concern. So, with no discipline there was no self-discipline. I caught him several times stealing money from Ann's handbag and made him return it. His attitude to a £10 note was 'Well she can afford it', hers, irritation that she had to take better care of her bag, mine that it was more than a week's wages.

Alien next-in-Line had been expelled from Westminster School for allegedly running an illegal gambling den but had settled well in to a local Comprehensive. Back living at home he now bathed daily but refused to change his clothes until they literally fell apart (God, that threadbare elbow less bluey green woollen jumper!). Bribery and cajoling were ineffective so enlisting the help of the renegade trio and their FSC inspired 'Mission Impossible' forays his clothes were delivered to the utility room and in the washing machine before he was out of the bath. Their rewards had to be discrete for fear of retribution.

The Female Alien was a special type of Alien. Having been a flouncing, petulant, obstreperous preteen princess she had become a sensitive, charming, funny and engaging teenager. In no small measure this had a lot to do with falling in love and being loved. Oh, we had a lot to thank Piers, and later, Jon, for over the next couple of years!

Following two weeks caravanning in Brittas Bay the long hot summer at Wiblings came to a close with Peter coming down to spend a week with me and the children. One déjà vu morning I found Peter and his four male children missing. The note on the breakfast table said *Back by lunch' 'Don't worry'*. Now where had I heard that before? This philosophy might be all right for the Indian mystic and Guru, Mehar Baba, who often used the expression "Don't worry, be happy" to inspire his disciples This facile advice was printed on inspiration cards and posters of the era but with Peter and missing children it was as useful to me as a trap door in a lifeboat. Vanessa, Jane and Emma over in the stables saddling up Piper, Zola and Cora, could not enlighten me.

'But I bet it's something that will make Ma mad' said Emma prophetically. How well she knew her father.

Never, in my worst nightmare did I imagine that Simon and Mark would return home the proud and ecstatic owners of air rifles. Jesus, Mary and Holy St. Joseph, there was no way I wanted to be within five miles of Wiblings when Ann came down at the week end. But looking on the bright side it could have been worse…he could have bought one each for John and Adam who were already swooning with envy.

To try to mitigate the consequence of his generosity he got Long Frank on side to set up rules for safe usage and to practice shooting at woodpigeons in the Copse. I made it plain they would not be on the menu at Wiblings so Frank would benefit from any carnage. Descriptions of Ann's response would be repetitious so I refer you back to the Doggy chapter. As usual I, did not escape blame nor did I have Peter's option of scarpering back to London.

'You should have phoned me as soon as you saw the guns, you're supposed to be in charge' she said appraising my performance as unsatisfactory. Hmm…

I don't think me being in charge was ever made plain to the Daddy.

Chapter 33

For whom the Bell Tolls.

When I was eight I had killed a bully of a Parish Priest. At least I thought I had killed him because I had made him apoplectic with rage by refusing to retrieve his golf balls as he had whacked them down Hession's field. A couple of weeks later he keeled over and died. Ergo it was my fault. Likewise, Emma had killed Opa. She had a friend to stay so looking for mischief they set about phoning people and engaging in absurd conversations. Penny, Emma's school friend was an accomplished mimic that could have given Joyce Grenfell a run for her money. Waiting for Oma to go out they put Opa on their tease list. Penny, pretending to be an outraged neighbour reported that Oma's chickens were chasing her cows and she wanted the problem dealt with forthwith. Giving Opa no opportunity to interject, or to even think about the preposterous idea of chickens chasing cows he set off in a state of great confusion to sort out the situation while they watched with glee. When they told me about his agitation I smiled in conspiracy because his unpleasantness had not lessened with age. A few weeks later the fickle finger of fate pointed to him and he died unexpectedly, making us all feel guilty, but Emma more so. I knew just how she felt.

His death and cremation in 1968 were low key non-events for the rest of the children. The three oldest had some fading memories of him teaching them to play croquet on the lawn, or card games on a wet day, but it was as if his disapproval of Ann's continued fecundity was visited on the younger children. Their only memories were of a frightening and disagreeable old man. To soften their impression of him Oma gave Ann the money to buy all of us a memento to remember him by. We chose between having radios or cassette players. My cassette player has been long overtaken by decades of new technology but Vanessa still plays her Bush radio. Adam, a kind-hearted child, was generous enough to add him to his nightly 'God Bless' list which also contained Rusty, Archibald, Barbara's feisty West Highland Terrier, and Oma's fit and friendly little whippet, Tina. Oma had introduced Tina to the household shortly after Rolo had gone to Doggy Heaven, Opa had put his foot down after Rolo's burial (where more tears were shed than at *his* last rites) issuing an edict that he was having no more barking dogs in the house. Oma might have been a dutiful wife, but she was no pushover, so found a fool proof way of circumventing his decree. She bought a whippet, the nearest thing to a non-barking dog on four legs. Personally, I think she should have got a Dobermann Pinscher but Tina made a wonderful family pet being obedient, patient, quiet, and tolerant. Whippets need a lot of exercise but Tina would get that by following Barbara and the girls out hacking or the boys out on their nefarious pursuits. They don't shed hairs, make fairly good watchdogs taking up a silent alert stance at unusual noises, but fall short on their guarding duties so Opa couldn't even complain about being growled at. Tina, in fact, showed no animosity towards him at all and often accompanied him on his daily constitutional, coming to heel when called, which I'm sure pleased him tho' he would never have admitted it.

For two years before Claud shuffled off to wherever St. Peter parked him, the children had been used to having parents living separately but under the same roof. They had therefore not had endure any of the traumas associated with the death knell of a marriage, and were not above manipulating events to their own advantage. Peter moving over to the Mews flat was so gradual it was hardly noticed. Once the flat had been upgraded it was expected that Peter would move in, but to recoup some of expense of renovation it was rented out to a well-heeled obnoxious American couple, who were the bane of my life, for six months. With complaints ranging from the lack of a heated loo seat to the narrowness of the Mews when manoeuvring their Shelby Cobra roadster into the garage they drove me insane. The former complaint I dealt with by telling Elizabeta to polish the toilet seat with Tiger Balm which warmed their bums for the rest of the day, the latter with a book on the History of the Royal Mews, persuading them that Her Majesty had to live with the same parking problem (Wow! Awesome!).

Even when he did move in Peter still came over to the playroom or had dinner at least once a week with Ann and the older children. I had a contact number for him when he was away overnight but his private life was just that, private. Although he and Ann no longer had a personal relationship they maintained an intellectual compatibility that made a parenting and professional relationship possible. It therefore came as a huge surprise early in 1969 to hear that divorce papers had been served. I wondered if she felt her father's boast that there had never been a divorce in the family no longer had to be respected now that he was dead, but I doubted that she cared that much about his opinion. Knowing Ann, I felt that what influenced her more was the thought of being disinherited. Ann was a total contradiction where money was concerned. She could be as parsimonious as my Gran, or generous to a fault. Refusing Anne Lingham and me a pay rise she bought Anne a state of the art electric typewriter and offered me a course of driving lessons. Neither of us had any doubt that the outcome of both of these acts of generosity would be of more benefit to her than to us. Anne's new typewriter would enable her to produce more work and its pristine professional finish would impress our clientele, and if I passed a driving test I could become the family chauffeur! However, as aul Annie Lawlor, a childhood neighbour used to say 'I *didn't come down with the last shower of turnips*' so I declined the offer. She had the same bipolar attitude to bills. I would pass all expenses on for her scrutiny before she moved them on to Diana to record them. I expected to be held to account for unforeseen expenses e.g. replacing the light shade broken in a clandestine game of football in the playroom. In this instance the shade went unremarked; instead she was clearly annoyed that I had replaced the 60-watt bulb with a 100 watt.

'And why was I always buying socks'?

I was tempted to write to Erle Stanley Gardner to ask him to put Perry Mason onto solving 'The Mystery of the Odd Sock Bag'.

Having told me about the forthcoming divorce Ann was not open to a discussion on the subject, just requesting that the children not be told until the case was heard. However, Oma was avid for news. She and I had developed a trusting relationship during our long days at the seaside or visits to the Roman dig at Bignor when she packed as many of us as she could into her Mazda Estate. I learned a lot about her early married life and how she chosen between her own happiness and her children, because, with Claud's influence in the Family Court, she was convinced she would have lost custody. Claud's boast was his way of reminding her that he had won.

'Divorce didn't stop him marrying me' she divulged.

'He knew my mother's first marriage was dissolved' but then I *did* come with a dowry' she added with a knowing nod and wry smile.

I respected her confidences in life so will say no more.

Due to the unhelpfulness of Ann's family's legal team, and Peters lack of interest in protecting his financial assets, his solicitor was tearing his hair out trying to collate information to put before the adjudicating judge. To aid a judge's decision to grant a divorce he or she must have all the information about both parties' income, expenses, property that they own, savings, insurance policies, pensions and shares etc. disclosed, and while Diana's booking skills were not forensic she uncovered several anomalies in the practice account which gave rise to concern. I was drawn into a murky world of sharp practice and questioned about my involvement with transactions associated with the children's school uniforms. I was aware that all educational expenses came out of a Trust Fund but now, under scrutiny it would seem that payments were coming out of Peters account but reimbursements were going elsewhere. Anne Lingham and Diana and I kept all discussion about finances amongst ourselves, while speculating about what form the grounds for divorce would take, the choices being;

Your spouse has slept with someone else and you find it difficult to carry on living with him or her ("adultery").

Your spouse has behaved in a way that makes you think you can't carry on living together ("unreasonable behaviour").

The Divorce Reform Act 1969 allowing couples to divorce after a separation of two years (five, if only one of them agreed) did not come into force until January 1971. A divorce could then also have been granted on the grounds that the marriage has irretrievably broken down, and it was not essential for either partner to prove "fault." If they had waited there would have been no need to wash dirty linen in public.

Imagine our gobsmacked surprise when the Evening Standard reported the Degree Nisi on the grounds of Ann's admitted adultery, and there wasn't even a hint of the Lady Anne. Not an iota of work was done as we had a speculation fest on whom, when and where. I don't think Ann gave any thought to preparing the children in the event of the news reaching them before she got home. It was Simon, then 18y and in residence having completed his A Levels, who broke the news at the tea table. I left him to the consequences of explaining adultery to the young and innocent while I reassured them that a divorce would make no changes to our lives, a rash but necessary statement at the time.

Chapter 34

Dedicated followers of fashion.

Childless Aunts very seldom get credit in their lifetime for the influence they have on their nieces and nephews' upbringing. Free from the obligation to rear children themselves they can become, for children, a benevolent adult to rely or, a surrogate mother when the need arises. Barbara, Ann's younger sister fulfilled both of those roles in the children's lives, including Vanessa's, and like all ungrateful little swine they took her kindness and tolerance for granted. I still remember her, as a lifelong companion to Oma, a daughter who tried to live in peace with her father and as somebody who naively saw no bad in anybody. She was sincere, honest and fair in all her dealings and polite to a fault. Having trained as a teacher her innate gentleness was no great asset so she changed the course of her life and joined Oma in setting up a local craft centre and becoming a renowned weaver. From the craft centre in Glasses grounds they **founded the Graffham Weavers Workshop and later organised craft camps for children.** Learning to weave was not a craft that enthused our lot tho' Vanessa still has a woven cushion cover that she made at one of the camps. The dozen or so participants camped in Barbara's field for several years where our motley crew joined them in FSC type camping activities. I was stressed out of my mind by Barbara's 'feed 'em, love 'em and leave them be' attitude waiting for a death or maiming to happen, but some of Beefy's teachings appeared to have permeated to the underused virtuous centre in their brains so visiting campers always went home alive and to give Beefy's Disciples their due they always used their Swiss Army knives with respect, well, apart from carving a few initials on trees.

Barbara was a country woman to the core. Her visits to London were brief, and apart from her time in Peru any time away from her own fire side was minimal. Surrounded by the beauty of the South Downs this was understandable. Also, keeping her close to Graffham was her livestock. Since returning to live at home in her early twenties she had always kept a horse, rode to hounds and traversed every bridle path along the South Down's Way until well into her sixties. Despite her buying a Shetland pony Simon and Mark showed no interest in riding when they were little so she had to wait for Emma to come along to share her enthusiasm. As a doting Aunt, this gave her an entrée into the exclusive group that was the Petworth Gymkhana Club set. Much to the chagrin of the local competitive mothers Emma, and later, Vanessa walked off with more than their fair share of rosettes. When John and Adam came along they too had no interest in horse riding so Barbara would now have to wait for Frances, Edwin's daughter to join her. With a father, allergic to horses I didn't hold out much hope.

   Barbara's enjoyment of the simple pleasures in life and lack of sophistication meant that she was tolerated by her more intellectual sister but like with Pops and Nan and Peter's sister Jean and her husband, any interaction was kept to a smiling but superficial minimum. It was my job to amuse them. A recurring example of this attitude to Barbara was Sunday lunch at Wiblings. Returning the girls from a mornings ride Ann would invite Barbara in for a pre-prandial drink. I had now taken over cooking the Sunday roast so knowing there would be plenty to go around I would sometimes invite Barbara to stay and eat. Well-seasoned to withstand Medusa type glares I would avoid looking at Ann, but her lack of verbal encouragement usually resulted in Barbara declining' If Barbara hesitated Ann would interject with an 'Oh, I'm sure Oma will be expecting her' which left Barbara in no doubt of her welcome.

Notwithstanding her benevolence, the children as soon as they were old enough to be embarrassed by adults shuffled off when they felt they had to entertain her. She had no fashion sense, wearing a selection of Nordic jumpers and Faroe Isle cardigans that Val Doonican would have coveted. Jodhpurs encrusted with horse and dog hair, riding boots that shed dried clumps of manure on carpets and an old Barbour coat of uncertain colour but a great comfort on a wet trek completed her usual ensemble. With prematurely greying hair that seldom crossed a hair dressers door and esqueing make up and depilatories her concession to dressing up to come to London involved woven tweed skirts, lisle stockings and sensible brogues. While not too out of place in West Dulwich our clientele and Ann's champagne socialist friends in W1 wore smart little Chanel suits or were encased in Mary Quant elegance while the more well-nourished chose Berketex. The only one to buck this trend was Ruth, one of Ann's old friends from Bodmin, who like Barbara, dressed for comfort.

To reflect their own fashion sense, our teenagers choose the hippie style, which dominated the decade. Bell bottom pants and denim jeans that were decorated with patterned beads or flowers became their clothing standard. Skirt styles were long and flowing, sometimes in tiers, and patched with brightly coloured material. Tie dye tops, psychedelic shirts and wide leather hipster belts were de rigour as were big floppy hats and granny sun glasses. It was the era of unisex fashion so Ophelia type flowing locks were grown by both sexes and held in place by beaded headbands. For those who forewent the headbands two curtains of hair gave them the English sheepdog look. Cotton kaftans and Jesus sandals were also to be found in both lots of wardrobes; however, Jesus beards remained the preserve of the male of the species. Having taught Emma to use a sewing machine she now came into her own making Quaker type smocks and floor length dirndl skirts. Dressing as they did I don't know how they had the gall not to make allowances for Barbara's eclectic outfits, whose classic style have actually stood the test of time. I hope when they look back at old photographs, and no longer stoned out of their minds, they ponder on what ridiculous followers of fashion they were.

And if they think I was ever fooled by the joss sticks think on!

Chapter 35

Skellingtons and Mystery Tours.

'Am I a Catlick or a Prodisan' Adam asked with his mouth full of Tayto crisps? We were on the train to Galway having spent the weekend with my Gran in Dublin where Adam had disappeared for the two days to play in the Square. It was October 1969, half term, and baking hot, the latter unheard of in Irish weather forecasters lore. As a result of packing for normal Autumnal seasonable weather we were both beaded in sweat as we stripped off our waterproof hooded anoraks and layers of clothing before tucking into a packed lunch. Being Irish I knew that woolen clothing was not made for the Irish climate - you'll get wet once and catch your death. The only Irish people who wear Aran sweaters are fishermen, non-swimmers all looking for a quick and merciful death if an Atlantic wave sweeps them out of their flimsy lath and tarred canvas currachs. Likewise, I didn't bother with an umbrella because it would turn inside out at the first gust of swirling Irish vortex type wind before it has the opportunity of protecting you from a drop of rain. 'Irish Weather' as a subject for philosophising is common. A greeting of 'fine soft day', 'God be with the hay makers', 'we need a fine harvest moon' or, for storm lashed fishermen, 'May God grant them a safe haven' are common ways of acknowledging the power of our weather on everyday life. We don't bother with seasons since the usual way to tell the difference between winter and summer in Ireland is to measure the temperature of the rain. In Dublin, the weather was gauged by whether or not you could see the Dublin Mountains; if you couldn't see them, it was raining; if you could see them rain was due!

One of the anomalies of the English Independent Schools and English National Schools systems was their freedom to decide the dates of their half term breaks. With seven children, all at different schools this inevitably meant that at least one of them would be 'home alone' for a week. It was easy if it was one of the girls, Barbara would be happy to have her, but John and Adam were a different shoal of herrings. John, going through his 'I want to be a chef' phase wasn't too bad provided he was let loose in the kitchen or could go across to the Planetarium nearby to gaze at the stars, but Adam wanted change, excitement, mystery and travel so when Ann purchased a freezer I did a cooking marathon, filled it with enough meals for a week and amidst much squawks of the u-n-f-a-i-r-n-e-s-s of it all took the opportunity to take Adam back to Galway.

'Why do you want to know' I asked in response to his question?

'Jimmy Grant said I must be a Prodisan because I'm English' he said scrutinizing the bottom of his crisp bag.

'And that when I die I will go to hell' he said in the same tone of voice he had just used to ask if I was going to eat my crisps.

Hmm…

Was I about to give him a resume of Irish History and feudal obligations from Strongbow to the Easter rising on three-and-a-half-hour journey? Was I hell!

'You're neither I told him.' They're football teams and you play rugby.

'Oh'…ok.

At 8y Adam's history class had probably just about covered the Roman Invasion, but 9y old Jimmy Grant's class had probably already reached the nineteen century *'an Gorta Mór'* His history was all around him from being able to count the strafing hits on the Dwellings by the Black and Tans in 1921 to the news on the tele that the British Troops were back on Irish soil in response to the Catholic Civil Rights Campaign in Derry. So, knowing your playmates loyalty was important. Being Irish or British was a base line, but being a Catlick or a Prodisan was the demarcation line.

The Rio Guest House was across the road from the Promenade in Salthill. It probably had sea views from some of its bedrooms, but ours was not one of them, however by the following morning a sea view was the least of my worries. On arrival, mid-afternoon we had gone for a long walk along the sea front Promenade in the sun returning to a spot near our guesthouse to watch the sun go down across the bay while eating our take away fried chicken and chips. Adam, exploring the rocky embankment where we were sitting, found, deep among the limestone boulders, the bleached skeleton of a Jack Russell terrier

The excitement of Howard Carter on discovering Tutankhamen's Tomb was as nothing compared to the ecstasy of an 8y old with his own skeleton. Sheltered from the elements, apart from the salt laden air, the terrier lay peacefully on its side with every bone in place down to the nails on its phalanges. 'Canikeepit, canikeepit, oh, p-l-e-a-s-e canikeepit said the finder echoing the calls of the eagle size seagulls wheeling over head hoping to swoop for the remnants of our meal.

Agreeing to help him disinter the remains I suggested it was best done the following morning because not having a camera he would have to draw a picture of how it looked for reassembly and we needed a container to collect all the bones. Reluctantly he agreed, ruminating the evening away with fears that somebody else would find this precious antiquity. He eventually went to sleep with an empty shoe box and pencil and paper by his bed courtesy of the lovely owners the Morris family. I, on the other hand, nearly died from dehydration during the night with food poisoning from the previous evening's fried chicken. En suite bathrooms were unheard of in most Hotels, never mind Guest Houses, so I locked myself in the first floor communal bathroom for the night, the loo serving one end and a waste paper basket the other, while the rest of the first floor guests trekked up to the second floor. Adam's gastrointestinal tract was totally unaffected thank heavens but he was less than sympathetic when told I couldn't go to the beach.

'I can go by myself' he pleaded beseechingly.

'It's only across the road' (he should have been an Estate Agent!).

'Sure the little peteen will be all right' Mrs. Morris assured me.

'We'll keep an eye on him while you get some rest'.

Amidst regular updates on 'the little peteen' I dozed the rest of the day away and rehydrated between regular trips to the bathroom. Eventually the intrepid disinterrer returned with a box full of bones and a handful of cutlery including a sugar tongs which had aided a successful excavation. It had taken him 8hrs. 8hrs in the sun and not a squirt of sun cream on him. Who on earth would bring sun protection to Galway in October? Luckily he'd been wearing shorts and a tee shirt, and with melanin laden genes didn't fare too badly. I, on the other hand, would have burned to a crisp. Having been invited to a family tea he spent the evening in the communal lounge entertaining the other guests who not only thought he was a little peteen, but a dote and a little treasure to boot.

One of our reasons for coming to Galway was so that he could go on another Mystery Tour. We were very nearly disappointed, the end of the holiday season being September for CIÉ, but with current hot weather the local coach drivers were taking advantage of the flock of tourists in town. Two of our fellow guests were taking a tour the next day, and, much to my relief agreed to take the peteen, because three hours on a coach without a loo was not altogether wise at that stage of my recovery. So, armed with map and a packed lunch he departed. Back at 5pm stuffed full of sweets, coca cola, ice cream and a pocket full of coinage all courtesy of his fellow venturers he was full of news, and twitchy as a meercat, from a surfeit of sugar.

'We went out along the Connemara coast road, across the Maamturk Mountains, down into Recess and home by Loch Corrib' he said spreading out his map.

'There are two other Mystery Tours' he informed me passing me a leaflet.

'Canwegoonthem, canwegoonthem, oh, p-l-e-a-s-e, canwegoonthem'?

'Sure the little jewel will be safe enough to go on his own if you're not feeling up to it' Mrs Morris said.

'We know all the drivers and I'm sure one of them would be happy to take him if you mention our name'.

Down on the Quay the following morning I was still uneasy about the prospect of a looless coach but decided to give it a go. It was obvious the drivers were taken with Adam. 'We'll look after him Mam if ye don't want to come' 'Sure the wee ladeen is not a ha'pert a bother, he'll be grand'.

'Are you going to the same places you went to yesterday' the ladeen asked his previous driver.

'Well me little Shulier' he said putting the butt of a cigarette behind his ear, 'If I told you that I'd have to kill ye'.

'But if oigh was going on a *Mystbery* Tour today oighed go for sure with ye'r man Seamus' he said pointing with his chin at a cheerful little barrel of a man shepherding several tourists onto his coach. Turfing a young German out of the front seat he told Adam to sit there where he could see him and could easily chuck him off if he annoyed him.

'We went down through Ballyvaughan to the Burren and the Cliffs of Moher *and I saw a bear's skelington'* said the owner of the again bulging pockets on his return.

'I told Seamus I had been there before with CIÉ but he said that wasn't a proper tour because there was no crack (craic) and they hadn't shown me the bear's cave'.

  For the non-Gaels amongst you 'craic' is hard to define as I found when Adam said he didn't understand what Seamus meant. I can only tell you that the essence of craic is in the talk and banter of good company, a group of people getting together to have a laugh and most of all to take a break from being serious about life. For CIÉ drivers' tours were a salaried job, with tips, so they had to make some effort to ensure the generosity of their passengers. But, for independent coach owners, tours were the difference between paying your bills and going hungry so they set out to gain custom by entertaining with myth, legend and music as well as providing a tourist spiel.

'Ger says we should go with him tomorrow because he's going somewhere I haven't been before'. Not being on first name terms with the drivers I had to assume Ger was Driver No.1 so feeling a lot better we both set off on Mystery Tour No.3. This one took in Leenane, Kylemore Abbey, lots of Lochs and finally Cong where 'The Quiet Man' was made. Both the Americans and Adam loved the latter, John Wayne being one of his favourite cowboys. I had great difficulty dissuading him from emulating the Yanks and buying a white Aran wool tam-o'-shanter for his mother and a shiny blackthorn Shillelagh for Peter. Instead he spent his loot on tooth rotting sticks of rock for everybody and was guided to buy his Mum a tasteful little Connemara Marble brooch.

His form teacher was less than thrilled to have a skeleton all the way from Galway produced for 'Bring and Tell', but his class mates were green with envy and could only have been more impressed if he'd found a dinosaur. I thought Mystery Tours would cure him of his 'Are we nearly there yet' habit but I hoped in vain. Once he knew where the destination was he continued to be a pain in the butt.

Chapter 36

Grist to the Mill.

'How long is it since you've filled in an Income Tax form' Ann's Accountant asked me.

Sitting across the table from him in Ann's Office cum Library he knew my response was going to be, 'Never', but continued with the charade anyway. In previous employment as a Probationer Nurse and then a Student Nurse any pittance of tax to be paid would have been deducted at source, and he was already aware of that since he was holding my P60 for 1960.

'So in the past nine years you have not claimed any allowances for you and your daughter' he enquired flashing the cufflinks on his handmade Jermyn Street shirt.

I may have been a total ignoramus when it came to Tax Returns but I knew his Saville Row suit, the shirt on his back, and his handmade Lobbs shoes were worth about five years' salary, my salary that is. I satisfied his question with a 'No' at which point he opened a folder and produced several pre-filled in Tax Returns.

'Unfortunately we can only reclaim six years of tax free allowances but you will find it worthwhile' he said smiling and steepling his fingers like Uriah Heep.

'We will of course have to calculate your salary in a different way to show the overall cost of your board and lodgings etc., and redefine your role both within the family and as an employee of the Practice'. Eh?

'Officially you will be Housekeeper to both, but your nurse training can be utilized within the Practice on a part time basis' he said as if offering me the Holy Grail. Hmm

I was already providing doughnuts for anorexics and a cuppa tea for our very illustrious early morning ECT patient, so was I going to usurp Archibald's role?

Was Archibald tax deductible?

Of course, he was. What a stupid question!

Now the Gran had ten commandments one of which was 'Never take Rubies from Swine' which I never fully understood until now, but I allowed this unctuous little creep to bamboozle me into signing the Returns on the assurance that there was nothing illegal in what I was doing, I would be participating in tax avoidance, not tax evasion, and both Ann and I would benefit from this arrangement. In other words, I would be doing what any money grubbing capitalist was doing, sheltering their income by paying as little tax as possible, and clawing back any taxable allowance going.

'*However*, (how did I know that there would be a however?) to balance yours and Ann's tax payments and tax allowance you will continue receive your current salary and nothing more, but Ann will undertake to put £400 a year in Trust for your daughter until she is old enough to receive it tax free in her own right, or until you leave her employment'.

Sounds fair enough, I wouldn't gain anything, Ann obviously would, and so would Vanessa, but I forget to factor in Ann's attitude to money which some years later led to a pivotal change in her professional life. Perhaps if she had followed my Gran's advice she would have saved herself an awful lot of grief.

Becoming a Housekeeper with two hats I also became an expert at scrutinising bills for deductibles as I learned to make Diana's life easier by separating Practice and household shopping. You'd be amazed what you can get away with under surgical supplies. Why the Revenue never queried the amount of female monthly sanitary wear claimed by a Psychiatric Practice is a mystery unless they thought we had a side-line in Gynaecology! They also never wondered if we were providing a Public Convenience the amount of loo rolls the Practice got through.

Chapter 37

Life shortening events and other sagas;

Some ten years or so after Peter had read my palm and told me I had a short life line I was writing to a friend of mine in Brazil who, over the years, was the recipient of a series of epic letters on family life, and I'm sure that there were times when he doubted both my veracity and my sanity.

Before updating him on 'The Fire' I reflected on other life shortening events and sagas he had been privy to, some of them already chronicled here. Those not yet mentioned so far come under the headings of;

The Missing Child
Talking To Strangers
'You Made Them Tea'?
Foreign Exchange
The Night at the Circus
Who Killed Cock Robin
The Dead Body
What Children?

~ ~ ~ ~

The Missing Child;

In Dulwich, when Vanessa transferred from Infant school to Primary School, on the same site, I stopped walking her to the school entrance, merely escorting her to the other side of Alleyn Park Road where she picked her friend Wendy up at her front gate on the corner with Bowen Drive and Wendy's Nan then watched them walk up the Drive into the school. Bowen Drive was a dog leg turning off Alleyn Park Road opposite our house so at the end of the school day I would cross the road and wait at Wendy's gate chatting to her Nan watching for them to hove into sight. John and Adam's school was a just across the road from our front garden and had a Lollipop Lady crossing so they usually waited with me on the pavement to watch her progress, or found their way into the house via the back door. One sun bleached day Wendy walked home alone. 'Where was Vanessa'? A shrug and a 'Dunno' came from 'not the brightest light in the harbour'. 'She didn't wait for me, so I came home alone' she reported looking grievously hard done by.

Leaving John and Adam with Wendy's Nan I ran up to the school quizzing classmates that I met. I found the Head getting out of her car to lock the gates behind her. 'No need to panic yet' 'she might be locked in the Toilet's' she told me with the guilty look of somebody who had not checked them before locking up.

Panic set in ten minutes later, when, with the aid of the school care-taker we had searched the entire school. I remember little of the activities of next hour as the Police unsuccessfully combed the area. Despite being at the height of the Brady-Hindley murder trial, abduction was way down the line of possibilities, running away from home, mischief, and thoughtlessness topping the list. I knew the first was highly improbable (because she would have inveigled one of the other two into going with her), and that if she prided her life the second was unlikely, but the third was feasible so where could she be? The question was answered just before 5.00pm when a police officer looking out the playroom window saw a child standing on the corner of Lyall Avenue. Knowing that crossing the road unescorted would incur my wrath Vanessa was waiting for somebody to come along to take her across. Accompanied by a very relieved sergeant she came up the front steps looking worried. I was so paralyzed with relief I could hardly move.

'Where have you been' I croaked, my voice cracking with tension as I hugged her.

'I've been to Theresa's to tea' she replied in voice that saw no problem in being missing for one and a half hours.

'Why didn't you tell me where you were going' I asked, not unreasonably?

I don't know whether it was the careless shrug or the blasé look that triggered a burst of fury, but in one fell swoop she was across my knee.

I only managed one ineffectual whack across her buttocks with Emma's pathetic plastic hair brush before it fell apart and she was rescued by one of the three policemen now sitting drinking tea in the playroom as they wrote up their incident report. While the Sergeant had a cautionary talk with the miscreant I sat and cried with relief. It transpired that Theresa's mother believed that I knew all about the invitation, but I still felt it remarkably careless of her for not checking, and for letting her walk home alone.

~ ~ ~ ~

Talking to Strangers

I watched my daughter like a hawk for several weeks to make sure she had learned her lesson, then one afternoon I saw Wendy walking home alone again. 'Where's Vanessa' I asked? 'She got into a car with a ban' she told me. Wendy had chronically enlarged adenoids and did a lot of mouth breathing which made her look half-witted and made some words difficult to enunciate, but you could say one thing about Wendy she didn't indulge in flights of fancy, so if she saw Vanessa getting into a car with a man that's exactly what happened. Jezzis wept!

I ran back home to phone the police to find the dastardly trio eating their after-school snack at the playroom table. Not a sign of guilt from the female one when asked how she had got home.

'Derek's Daddy gave me a lift' said she, unconcerned, not bothering to take her eyes off 'Pussy Cat William' on the television. "The clock it ticks, the clock it tocks" went the theme tune. I'm not sure how many lives William had at this point, but she was down to about five.

'What had I told them about strange men' Looking puzzled they recited the warnings verbatim

'But he's Derek's Dad' Vanessa explained, the other two agreeing like two papier-mâché nodding dogs, 'He's not a s-t-r-a-n-g-e man, he's D-e-r-e-k's Dad' they explained as if I was being particularly moronic.

Derek's Dad, or not, he had chosen to give my daughter a lift home, so why not Wendy as well? In this day and age, it would be highly suspicious, but apart from warning the three of them never to get into any car without me knowing about it I left it at that. Had I got the concept of strange men across?

Did they know keeping secrets was bad? Did they know that if anybody touched them and they didn't like it they should tell me? Well their understanding was soon put to the test. Coming through the Kingswood Estate on his way to see Peter, our GP, Dr. Gottlieb, whom the children knew well, stopped to offer Vanessa a lift and was told she was not allowed in a 'strange man's' car. John was hurt playing rugby and was told to leave the pitch and sit in the school van with the driver until the game had finished. He refused, sitting in the rain rather than get into a vehicle with a 'strange man'. Adam came to tell me that Tip had patted him on the head. I despaired of them ever reaching an understanding of a danger, still regarded as unlikely, but grasp it they did so that several years later when John was groped in the Victoria Cartoon Cinema the three of them immediately moved seats and told the usherette.

~ ~ ~ ~

'So You Made Them Tea'?

My own gullibility was put to the test in a mortifying way when I was interviewed by the local constabulary in connection with our neighbours at No.45 in Dulwich. While our relationship with Col. Townsend, at No.49, was somewhat cool we had none at all with the Jones's who had bought the freehold of the plot at No.45 having gone for architectural modernism to replace bomb damaged Victoriana. Their flawless front lawn and neat flower borders were flaunted for the passing world to see and for passing burglars to reconnoitre. Removal day dawned hot and sunny a large removal van backed into the drive. As the day, progressed Anne Lingham and I ruminated on the fact that the family had hardly given the house a chance before moving on, and were not even bothering to oversee the house being emptied. The removal men stripped off and lay out in the sun for their lunch break, made small talk with the children, and had frequent tea breaks. I got involved when they ran out of tea and got chatted up to replenish the supply. They left at their leisure. Several days later the police called to ask if we had seen anything of a gang of thieves who had stripped the house next door while the family was on holiday! I remember little of the interrogation apart from the fact that a smug young constable kept repeating 'Let me get this straight you made them tea'? This was factually incorrect but I was too embarrassed to argue. The only help I could give was to tell them the gang were not East Enders because having spent three years in E3 I knew a Cockney Sparrow when I heard one.

~ ~ ~ ~

Foreign Exchange

As the older children became teenagers Ann used family contacts to set up exchange visits in France and Germany to improve the children's language skills. In return, several times we had the delightful Rémy from Caen in Normandy, the pleasant linguistic sister and brother, Ursula and Christian, from Heidelberg and the truly vile Christopher from Paris, the latter only once. At a time when Peter was still having some of his meals with us keeping him, and them, apart took a bit of juggling. He was never the most sociable of people therefore eating a meal with strange teenagers was not part of any wish list, and eating a meal with strange foreign teenagers was the equivalent of ending up in fifth circle of hell. It became more problematic when we moved to WI because there was a serving hatch between the kitchen and dining room and Peter often spoke before checking the latter. So, our exchange students had to endure such inquires as
'Is the Norman invasion over'?
Are those krauts still here'?
I tried to make a game out of it blaming the British sense of humour and promising them a jar of Sainsbury's chocolate spread or a bottle of Heinz Tomato Ketchup (both firm favourites) to take home for every

time they heard the word kraut or frog. Ursula and Christian won hands down and clambered to come back again. Dad's Army, when it started in '68 was a great hit with them, however 'Allo 'Allo and Fawlty Towers had still to grace our TV screens.

Christopher would return over everybody's dead body including Elizabeta's. 'He is a filthy smelly foreigner' said our foreign cleaner. `Que você deve olhar em seu quarto, é um porco repugnante'.

He was in fact using Mark's room, and a revolting little cochon he was. The smell from the room was a mixture of unwashed clothes, Andouillette sausage and musk from sheets that I did not care to examine.   Mark had deliberately gone hiking in Scotland with his school so that he didn't have to entertain him. A week in Paris with Christopher and his family had been enough to convince him that he never wanted to see Christopher again, but we were stuck with our end of the bargain. I use the Royal we here but I was the one left to look after him for a week. I'm sure that over the years he has turned into a charming, good looking articulate man, but as a boy in his mid-teens he was the pits. His long greasy hair, pimples, granny glasses and seedy gothic ensemble were not impressive. But it was his Gallic shrug, mumbling, and unwillingness to converse in any language that drove me to the edge of insanity

'Ce qui vous aiment faire'?

Gallic shrug

`Où aimez-vous aller

Gallic shrug

Le `tout près là est le zoo, Madame Tussauds, le planétarium?

'Mumble…

Eventually he hands me a tourist map and says 'Ruka Arnabe'

After an exhaustive question and answer session I discovered that the only place this shambling wretch wanted to see was Carnaby Street.

I was so relieved to get him out of the house I actually walking him there pointing out The Souk on the way. It is me his mother can thank for the rank Afghan goat skin coat he bought in the latter.

He was supposed to live en famille but nobody would eat with him because of his disgusting table manners.

Ahh, memories, memories…

Memories, light the corners of my mind,
Misty watercolour memories of the way we were'

Matters came to a head several mornings into his stay. He and Peter were the only ones at the breakfast table, Peter behind the Guardian, Christopher slurping café au lait which he had helped himself to from Peter's percolator. The disgusting sound was sufficient to make Peter lower his paper just as the pigeen dipped his buttered toast into a cereal bowl full of coffee (don't ask) and shoehorned a huge wodge of the greasy pap into his Gaping Gill of a mouth. Peter didn't hang about for the mastication, the drooling rivers of butter down the chin or the licking of the fingers, he was head down over the kitchen waste disposal unit reuniting himself with his own coffee and toast. It was sufficient revenge for our recent night at the Circus.

~ ~ ~ ~

The Night at The Circus;

One of Peter's patients owned a Ticket Agency so we were occasionally the grateful recipients of Ballet, Opera, Theatre, Pantomime or Circus tickets. Our latest night out had been to see the Circus at Earls Court. I think only the trio had come, but Jane may have been there as well. The children and I had travelled by Tube expecting Peter to take us home in his new car. In his very new car, a car, he had only taken delivery of that very day. We came out of Earls Court, umbrella less in the pouring rain. 'Just across the road' said the proud owner of the new car. Walking up and down the road produced no Triumph 13 bottle green car but several cranky shivering children. The car had been stolen.

'What's the number plate' I asked.

A shifty twitch of the shoulders and a failure to make eye contact confirmed he hadn't a clue.

'Wewannagohome, wewannagohome, wewannagohome n-o-w' wailed the new car owner's dripping offspring.

Hailing a passing Panda car Peter reported the car stolen. The two constables therein deserve a prize for diplomacy, and for managing to keep a straight face when told we didn't have a number plate. Just in case they were dealing with the criminally insane one of them asked me quietly if we were all ok, encircling the children in his glance. When they got a resigned affirmative nod, they wound up their windows to keep the rain out and departed promptly, suggesting we phoned the nearest police station when we could supply the number plate. Two days later the car was found exactly where he parked it, liberally decorated with parking and penalty tickets because he had forgotten to display his 'Disabled Driver' disc. On arrival, he had parked it near the Earls Court Tube entrance, but the rest of us had gone in via the West Brompton entrance and that's the one we all used to exit. He and I had a very petulant conversation about mind reading.

Him; 'Was he supposed to be a mind reader to guess I would use the West Brompton exit'?

Me; 'Nooo, but he could have taken note of the entrance he used to come in… and the name of the road in which he had parked the car… and the number plate… and if his mind reading skills were as flaky as his palm reading attempts then we'd still be standing in the rain by the feckin roadside'.

While we had been waiting to meet up at the Circus I had paid a visit to the booth of a bona fide Gypsy fortune teller who had predicted that I had a long life ahead of me and that my Prince Charming lived in Never-Never Land. Both true. I was tempted to suggest to him that he take up Alectromancy as a side-line. I even knew where he could find a rooster.

~ ~ ~ ~

Who Killed Cock Robin?

Keeping an eye on Simon and Mark as they became teenagers was difficult. Simon, we only saw during school holidays and initially the same could be said of Mark, until he was expelled from Westminster and sent to a day school. At Wiblings they were teenagers with guns.

They were roaming teenagers with guns.

They were teenagers with guns that I wouldn't trust if my life depended on it. Charmingly devious teenagers with guns who assured me they were keeping to the rules and only killing vermin.

So, who was responsible for the massacre in the Copse?

An incandescent Frank turned up with four pathetic multi-coloured limp little bodies. In any broad-leafed wood spring migrants include black caps, chiffchaffs, nightingales, pied flycatchers, willow warblers, and redstarts. There are usually lots of members of the tit family all year around, as are tree pipits, tree creepers, woodcock, wood pigeon, wood warblers and all three species of woodpecker so the nearby copse was well endowed down to its own cuckoo.

While the woodcock and wood pigeon could be regarded as food, none of the rest, by the widest stretch of the imagination, could be classed as such, and definitely not as vermin. As luck would have it, Peter was down for several days enjoying the sun and some time with the children so I left him to deal with Frank while I phoned Ann. I know I had a major crisis on my hands so I was ensuring no blame would fall on me, forgetting that when shit hits a fan it splatters *everybody*. 'Why hadn't I put Frank on the phone to her, so that she could contain the situation'? Telling her Frank was more interested in a flogging than diplomacy was a waste of breath. So, what did she want me to do? Was she coming down? Was she hell! 'Put Peter on' she told me.

Ten minutes later the three of them had decamped for London leaving me to deal with a savage Frank, distraught Oma and a furious Barbara and the cold looks of villagers as the other children and I did our weekly sweet shopping. Graffham had an enviable grapevine which must have stood them in good stead during WW2.

~ ~ ~ ~

The Dead Body;

And if the massacred birds were not enough to contend with I soon had a real dead body to worry about. Returning from trekking in Scotland, Mark and his friend Ginger, while consuming a repast like starving gannets, informed me they had found a body down a gulley. Agog to find out the consequences of their discovery they informed me, between chomps, there were no consequences because they had not reported it! What? Why? Jezzis!

'Because the Fuzz would have kept us there for hours' the Ginger one unashamedly told me'

'We had to keep going to keep up' a repentant looking Mark added.

Since both of them were old enough to have married at Gretna Green I believed they were also old enough to have a responsibility towards others, to regret what they had done, and for me to tear strips off them and leave them in no doubt that their behaviour was reprehensible. However, as far as I know the shredding and emotional blackmail was in vain and the body still remains unshriven and undiscovered in a Scottish wilderness.

~ ~ ~ ~

'What Children'?

The same two villains were about on the evening the house caught fire. When last seen, they had been sitting at the dining room table. About an hour later I was alerted to the fact that there was something wrong when Mark came thundering down the basement stairs late one evening and ran back past me with a fire extinguisher, panting 'Fire' before disappearing upstairs. The basement was fireproofed from the rest of the house so undoing the fire exit door into the front Area I left Adam sleeping while I went to investigate using the internal stairs through the fireproof door into the hall. The front door was wide open but not a sign of smoke on the ground floor, first floor likewise. On the second floor, the fire door separating the family quarters from the Practice was held open by an empty fire extinguisher allowing the wind from the open hall door to blow a pillar of smoke straight up to the children's bedrooms on the top floor. Peter and Mark were fighting a losing battle with a second set of full length curtains on one of the windows in the dining room the first set now a blackened sheath of burned silk.

'Had the Fire Brigade been called?

Eliciting a 'Yes' I started closing doors to stop the smoke damage spreading assuming that Ann had already removed the children from the scene, but I thought I'd check with Peter before venturing to the top floor.

'What children' he asked blue in the face with coughing spasms?

Er... Emma, Jane, John and Vanessa?

Er...no they were still in bed.

This was when I finally decided that Psychiatrists should never be allowed to procreate.

   Bounding up the stairs I found four closed bedroom doors, a landing full of smoke and all four of them blissfully unaware of anything being amiss. Emma and Jane were still awake but rousing John and Vanessa wasn't easy. Emma did a brilliant and capable job shaking the life out of them while I unsuccessfully tried to open the Fire Exit door to the roof. As a cost cutting exercise this had not been renewed during the renovation so was prone to stick. It was now so warped I didn't have the strength to push it open. Both Jane's and Emma's windows opened on to a narrow, railed, ledge on the roof, which formed part of the fire escape route, but opening them would further funnel the smoke along the landing. It wouldn't be my exit of choice but I had just committed to it when two Cybermen appeared through the smoke. On closer examination, they turned out to be fire-fighters in breathing apparatus. Making short work of the warped door we were out on the roof, me, noting as I traversed the fire escape route the amount of tokers discarded spliff ends, then we were on the next-door roof and in through the Greatorex's fire exit to be received with polite lukewarm British hospitality never having been formally introduced to them.

Adam, still snug and safe in the basement, was filled with envy, which was to some degree dissipated when the fire crew allowing him and Archibald to sit in the cab while they wound up their hoses and tried to discover the seat of the fire. During the next morning's post mortem the damage to the house was revealed. The fire which had started by the dining room curtains remained a mystery tho' the investigating officer showed considerable interest in the cigarette butts found three floors down in the front Area. However, pre-DNA they did not amount to evidence so we were left with an Act of God, or spontaneous combustion, probably regarded as the same thing, but the Insurance paid up anyway. The original murals in the dining room were smoked damaged as were the brocaded chairs but the fire had remained localised by the windows so the long teak table recovered well with a good oiling. It was the water damage caused by the fire that was so horrendous. The parquet floor in the dining room would have to be replaced and the floor and ceiling in the grand drawing room underneath renovated. It was the latter that had the most damage from the cascades of water from fire hoses from above. It took several days for the house to dry out and for life to regain a semblance of normality. Everything and everybody reeked of smoke. We has all suffered some degree of smoke inhalation but Emma suffered the most having had to cross the landing several times to rescue the others while I struggled with the door so she was hoarse for days.

There had been something niggling at me that suddenly came to the surface as Ann and I sat going through curtain patterns.

'Where were you on the night of the fire' I asked.

I was here' she said indicating the drawing room where we were sitting.

'Where were you when I went upstairs to get the children?

'I had to run to The Clinic to dial 999 (The London Clinic on the corner, *and the reason for the wide-open hall door*).

'What was wrong with our phones?

'They were both dead'.

Having endured a portion of blame for every catastrophe that had ever befallen the household I was totally blameless in this instance, apart from not ratting out the smokers. The fault lay at her door or rather at the hall door she left open to run along the street to use a phone when we had two working phones in the hall.

Yes, two working phones which could be switched to the hall with the depression of a button. Hmm…

I decided that revenge would be sweet but too short-lived to enjoy, so allowed her to discover in time the consequences of feeding a fire and how to switch the phones through to the hall.

Chapter 38

Lovers and Rovers.

In the two years following the divorce life went on more or less as before except that Peter came upstairs to eat less frequently. This made little difference to Simon and Mark who were invited over to the Mews on prearranged evenings to play chess. In their late teens, and with new legislation entitling them to vote, they were now also considered old enough to share a bottle of wine or two. Emma and Jane certainly saw less of him but he still appeared in the playroom to observe John, Vanessa and Adam's table tennis matches. Pop, his father, had died shortly before the divorce so Nan, then in her mid-seventies, stopped travelling to see us. Instead, over the next couple of years he took me and the trio down to Plymouth a couple of times to visit her and to catch up with his sister Jean and her two boys, Paul and David. To be factually correct we made one leg of the journey by train since *he* seldom stayed longer than one night.

His relationship with the Lady Anne continued with little impingement on family life. Emma, a gregarious, outgoing, bright teenager doing well academically, seemed unaffected by the changes within the family and had a wide circle of friends. Jane, a very pretty, thoughtful, considerate girl, was a polar opposite. I don't remember her ever bringing a friend home, and her introversion cloaked a struggle to keep up with course work. She relieved her stress by developing trichotillomania, an impulse control disorder, which resulted in her plucking out all her eyelashes and an ever-growing golf ball sized bald patch behind her right ear. Trying to prevent her going into a trance-like state and pulling out her hair and lashes while watching television increased her distress and anxiety. This created tension in our relationship and she became the silent Jane of old. However, with both parents unwilling to acknowledge that she needed cognitive behaviour therapy to control the symptoms there was little I could do in my state of ignorance, except nag her when I couldn't divert her, which just added to her problems. Ann was quite keen to put any failure to improve at my door, but short of putting Jane's hands in boxing gloves, without treatment there was little to accomplish. A less demanding school might have helped, but a mother's determination that with money and clout, her children would be high flyers would have to be overcome. The only one to escape this pigeon holing was John, who having done well at Sewardstone School's specialist dyslexic stream was now boarding at Seaford College in Graffham, where like the former; there was recognition that an education was more than exam results. However, he would have been a lot happier at home. Keeping his tuck box replenished for him was poor recompense for missing out on home life.

Outside the house the country was in turmoil. The Miners' Strike, inflation at a 30-year high, hundreds of Asians arriving from Uganda and the escalating trouble in Northern Ireland exported to the mainland was a flavour of the time. Despite it all patients came rolling up. Home-grown and foreign Royalty, Aristocrats and plutocrats, Maestros and Rock Gods, the Literati and the Glitterati all withstood Archibald's scrutiny apart from the home-grown Royal who was discretely visited at Kensington Palace. Most doctors who treat the Royal Family end up with a Knighthood but Peter did not expect an honour knowing royal psychiatrists would never be acknowledged.

Amelia was still with us, and still demanding an annual pay rise commensurate with inflation. In the early days, she had been with us for several months before I cottoned on to her scam. At 7.00am she started with us. Proving herself trustworthy and reliable she had been entrusted with the front door keys so I would hear her clattering about, usually well before her official start time. Being in demand locally her jobs went on until 7.00pm. Saturdays she arranged a specialist yearly spring cleaning employing family members to climb ladders to dust mouldings, re hang curtains and move furniture. She went through so much bees wax polish it's a wonder she didn't keep her own bees. It was Elizabeta who alerted me to the fact that something wasn't quite kosher. Seldom actually seeing Amelia I left a message with Elizabeta to give to her when she saw her in passing at 9.00am. The message remained undelivered for several days until I discovered that they're paths seldom crossed because Amelia had long gone by Elizabeta's start time. Poor Elizabeta was quaking with trepidation worrying that she had got her Aunt into trouble. She explained Amelia's scheme. Amelia overlapped all her jobs by about 30 minutes. We paid her from 7.00 to 9.00am while the Dental Practice across the road paid her from 8.30 to 10.30am and so on to her last job of the day from 5.00 to 7.00pm. Was I going to tell Ann? No. Amelia was a great worker. She turned up hail rain or shine. I couldn't fault her work, and the way I looked at it, if she wanted to leave early in lieu of a coffee break than that was up to her. So, I turned a blind eye, and only Elizabeta and I ever knew how she worked the system.

By 1972 Ann's Practice was well established and she had taken control of her personal appearance losing nearly four stone since the divorce. Down in size to a Marks and Spencer 16 (long) she could now buy off the rack. At 44y she was a handsome woman and with a honey blonde rinse to cover strands of gray was ready to go back on the circuit.

With the aid of a Weight Watchers Cookbook I could have, by then, completed a Master's Degree in 500 Calorie Meals. Rather than lunch elsewhere and have to worry about what to order she took to inviting personages to lunch at home. From an established network of friends I got to meet some very interesting and influential women. I could name drop for the next couple of pages but my favourite, and only male invitee, was George Mickes. George was a Hungarian writer and broadcaster. He was the author of a brilliantly funny book poking fun at the English called "How to be an Alien". It had a one line chapter on Sex; "Continental people have sex lives; the English have hot-water bottles." One of my favourite quotes was; "The world still consists of two clearly divided groups: the English and the foreigners. One group consists of less than 50 million people; the other of 3,950 million. The latter group does not really count".

George liked a little siesta after lunch so would take himself off to the sofa in the children's dining cum sitting room.

With strict instructions to wake him after half an hour we would sit and talk with him quizzing me on what I found strange or amusing about the English being, as I was, a 'foreigner' in an English house. He also quizzed me about Irish proverbs, and sayings of my Gran and the other women in the Dwellings. He was particularly interested in their understanding of the 'nagers'. Hungarians have long had a reputation for being the gloomiest nation in Europe. They are renowned for their pessimism, melancholia and despair, and suicide seems to be part and parcel of Hungarian culture. 'A Hungarian who hasn't got a relative or friend who haven't committed suicide is a rarity' he told me. Despite his wit and jollity, I felt he understood the dangers of melancholia quite well. He also told me that the song 'Gloomy Sunday' by Rezső Seress, and sung by Billy Holliday, among others, was known as the Hungarian suicide anthem because its impact was so lethal that many people were said to commit suicide to it, or leave the lyrics with their farewell notes. The composer himself unsuccessfully attempted to take his own life by jumping out of a window but later in the hospital choked himself to death with a wire. The tune is strangely haunting, and the lyrics capture a yearning for death.

"Little white flowers won't wait for you,
not where the black coach of sorrow has taken you.
Angels have no thought of ever returning you.
Would they be angry if I thought of joining you?"

Ann, having shed so much weight and feeling good about herself had had very little success cultivating any meaningful male relationship. At somebody's suggestion she joined a social network for professional unattached people. The organisation provided a venue for social events to enable like-minded seekers to meet compatible members but she found the male/ female ratio discouraging. However, she enjoyed the social events so persevered until she met somebody she found interesting.

And so, it was that Philip entered our lives and with him an era of family life came to an end. Initially we saw little of him at Devonshire Place but Wiblings was a different matter. He gradually progressed from going down to Sussex for the day on Sundays to staying for the weekend. I cannot speak for anybody else, but his attempts at goodwill fell on stony ground with me, particularly when he took over cooking the Sunday lunch. Calorie counting fell by the wayside as a surfeit of cholesterol was introduced and Ann's hard won battle losing weight was undermined to the extent that the pounds began to creep steadily back on. Very soon I was spending my weekends in London with whatever children were home. Their reluctance to spend weekends with the happy couple was marked by their lack of enthusiasm to travel to Graffham on Fridays. My staying in London initially didn't go down well with Emma, who, having outgrown horses was into entertaining and was used to having her friends over. Stoned and happy they smoked, sunbathed on the roof fire escape, and having put the world to rights departed without trace on Sunday afternoons. Having no cause for concern I stayed downstairs leaving them to enjoy their freedom and thanked Searle for the Pill. However, I had my uses when it came to producing vats of curry and spaghetti Bolognese. Vanessa still went down to Wiblings, primarily for the opportunity to ride, but now stayed with Barbara. John a weekly boarder at Seaford College nearby preferred to stay with Oma, who having sold Glasses to a member of her family, was living in a personally designed much smaller house in the grounds, with an entrance just beyond Barbara's cottage. Adam stayed with me and we usually went to the cinema. Back then you could buy a ticket and watch the film several times over. With Adam home Archibald stayed too.

When the trio were in London together they reverted to seeking their own diversions. It was possible to buy a rover ticket to travel anywhere by bus or underground around Central London for a day. Saturday evenings were spent planning which involved much searching of routes and maps. Special themes were chosen. One week all stations they were going to alight at on a chosen route must have the word 'Park' in it, another week it might be 'Green' or 'Square' or contain the name of an animal, so stations such as Elephant and Castle, Blackhorse Road or Goldhawk Road were chosen. Bus routes were picked in a like manner except it was particular bus stops that were designated. The venturers had no interest in tourist routes; their obsession was with orienteering and progressed to finding the quickest routes. I often wondered if they were ever disappointed when they reached their stop offs with exotic sounding names to be confronted with mundane reality. Sundays saw them departing with their packed lunch and maps in their mini rucksacks. Success was initially measured in achieving their mission but real enjoyment later progressed to aiming for the shortest routes and cutting time off the journey. Little did I think that two of them would make a career out of route planning!

Chapter 39

Footprints in the sands of time.

Åsa Briggs Report on 'The Future of Nursing and Midwifery' not only changed the face of nurse training but also opened possibilities for nurses, who like me, had not had the opportunity to complete their training. The then current rules stipulated that if I returned to nursing I would re-enter training at the Preliminary Examination stage of 15months plus a month would be deducted for every year I had been out of the system. This meant that at this stage, I would have to recommence the three-year training with only 3months credit, a daunting prospect.

Professor Briggs proposed that anybody who had passed the Preliminary Examination should be allowed to re-enter training on an accelerated 18month course. This amounted to 78 weeks. Sam and his wife had been urging me for several years to come and live with them while I completed my training, so the option could now become a reality. With Adam destined for boarding school in September, and changing circumstances in the family I gave it serious consideration. It would mean going to live in Radlett in Hertfordshire. Radlett was on the St. Pancras to Bedford British Midland mainline route. With a free schoolchild travel pass Vanessa could remain at Haverstock School for her Secondary education by travelling into Kentish Town but I would only have two possible hospitals I could train at without too much difficulty; 'The Royal Free' in Grey's Inn Road near St. Pancras, or 'St. Alban's General' travelling in the opposite direction. 'The Free' being a teaching hospital was the more prestigious but also more difficult to get in to.

I told Peter my plans. He agreed it was a good time for me to go but entreated me to tell him the outcome of my application before I informed Ann because he wanted the opportunity to be incommunicado. Agreeing, I pointed out to him that in the circumstances he would have to be my referee so we would need to include Anne Lingham in my intention.

Within a week I had an interview with Rosemary Bailey, Matron of 'The Free'. Holding Peter's fulsome and embellished reference, and a glowing but unexaggerated one from my previous Matron, Grace Laing, she offered me a place in the September Set. I was speechless with delight. I was also mightily relieved because it gave me nearly four months to make plans and see Adam off to Boarding School. The latter relief was short lived. Before I got around to telling the select few I had a phone call from 'The Free's' Principal Tutor Thelma Berry telling me that a candidate had dropped out of the next Set and she was offering me the place. '

'When is the start date' I asked in trepidation, and with fingers crossed? 'Well, the Block starts the end of May…three weeks hence'. Oops…

Ann hardly spoke a word to me for the next three weeks excluding me from participating in finding a replacement. Feeding her obvious ire was the discovery that a new housekeeper was going to cost her at least three times my salary. She would also need to define hours and designate days off. This was going to be a whole new ballgame. Simon, and Mark were away at University and Emma was preparing to go so they were quite blasé about my departure, while Jane was too stressed out over 'O Levels' to care. John's main concern was who was going to be responsible for his tuck box. Adam would miss me, but with the Pizza Hut franchise now established and a freezer full of food he'd cope. And Vanessa? Well I was ruining her life, wasn't I? Or as kids say today 'Init'.

So, after 13 years of a life lived and shared I left the house with two weeks wages and a handshake from Ann. Peter's generosity on the other hand meant I could start my training with a complete set of Nursing Books and a Rail Pass from Radlett to St. Pancras for a year. While I did not doubt his generosity, I was sure the aptness of his gifts was down to Anne Lingham, otherwise God alone knows what he would have chosen!

In contrast when Amelia left she did so having built three holiday villas on the Algarve to ensure a comfortable old age.

When my day of departure came, I went, with regret, knowing that our destinies would once again be thrown on life's surge as we set out on our individual journeys. Since then two lives in the family have tragically been cut short, one choosing to thread a path of no return; another surrendered his health to fate. Life however has smiled kindly on the rest of us and their story is not mine to tell.

I Dreamt I Dwelt in Marble Halls.

~ Synopsis ~

The rent of 3s.6d a week in the Dublin Artisans' Dwelling Company flats was relatively high in the early 1920's when the author's grandparents moved in. Built to house artisans the tenancies were beyond the means of labourer's who earned about a £1 a week.

On the death of her mother in 1947 she moved from nearby Upper Rutland St. to live in the Dwellings with her grandparents and remembers it as a matriarchal enclave where the women castigated and cursed each other's children and minded them when necessary. They criticized one another, supported one another through the 'nagers', delivered babies when a 'Bona Fide' midwife wasn't available or couldn't be afforded, borrowed and lent finery, often taken out of the Pawn for the occasion, and laid out and waked the dead. The Memoir is rich in humour and historical lore for those who remember Summerhill, the Dwellings, the nearby Streets, the Tin Church, and the choice of schools like the Red Brick Slaughter House, the Sado Brothers or the love 'em or hate 'em Nuns in North William Street. It will lead you down a path of nostalgia you cannot fail to enjoy. For others, it's a series of glimpses of North Dublin communal life that for once does not include vermin, abuse, neglect or a granny who was a dealer. It also encompasses vignettes of family members bringing them to life to be remembered fondly with wry recognition of their faults and foibles. We are introduced to characters like Annie Lawlor, Nick Colgan and the Grant and Breslin families and will meet some of them again in 'Thrown on Life's Surge'.

The Summer Children

~Synopsis~

This book is a memoir of long summer holidays the author spent in Claregalway with her mother's family from 1944 to the mid 1950's. Living in an inner-city area in Dublin this annual holiday was like another world where she, and her two siblings, ran free and wild ignoring edicts to keep away from the river, stay out of the field with the bull in it, not to eat or drink anything from Bina Lenihan's kitchen and not to annoy the neighbours. Lying about these activities was enough to ensure that she, and her co-conspirators, had sufficient sins to make a weekly confession worthwhile.

As self-centred children, they were not aware of the struggles and sacrifices of their hardworking family who farmed the land and slaned the turf in the townlands of Gortcloonmore, Gortadooey, Montiagh, Cregboy and Cloonbiggen, the latter in the townland of Claregalway, all, within the Parish of Claregalway.

Today the old Claregalway townlands are little more than names on a map vying for space with new housing estates, and a simple way of life has long gone. Local characters are remembered by fewer and fewer people but for those who do remember them they are recalled with great affection.

In an era when people stopped for the angelus bell and when money only changed hands on Fair and Quarter Days neighbour harvested with neighbour, divided butchered meat and Hughes Shop put weekly necessities 'on the ledger' until customers had the where-with-all to settle the account. Living as we do now in money and possession driven times a look back on a simpler life is a salutary experience. As her Dublin Gran was wont to say 'You don't know where you're going unless you know where you've been' so as this memoir unravels the tricks of memory and fable, it records both sad and happy times. There is mischief aplenty, music galore, waking the dead, tales of Canon Moran and family skeletons.

Thrown on Life's Surge
~ Synopsis ~

This memoir is part of an Irish trilogy based on the experience and recollections of the author, a Dublin girl from Summerhill, a decaying north inner city area a short walk from the City Centre. Her first volume provides a glimpse of a Dublin childhood and family life in the Artisans Dwellings, Upper Buckingham Street in 1940's -1950's Dublin, and the second, in complete contrast, an account of running wild in the boglands of Galway during the long summer holidays. This volume covers the period of a nurse training course at St. Anne's Skin and Cancer Hospital. There, age 17y, she learned to deal with the terminally ill on a daily basis in a setting that provided dignity, comfort, camaraderie and, more surprisingly, fun.

The Nuns, her fellow probationers and the patients are all portrayed as people well remembered. The Nuns range from the 'She Devil' to the saintly and the probationers as culchie's to the core, united in their urge to escape bondage on the family farm. Stories of the patients are poignant, in particular those of Mikeen and Maggo. In contrast the humour of the deaths of Mrs. Von and the Widow Maker, and the hilarity of a Day at the Races is life affirming and funny.

Pea Soup and Jellied Eels
~ Synopsis ~

The scene changes from the Dublin of the previous trilogy as the author arrives in Poplar in 1957 to train as a nurse in St. Andrews Hospital in Bromley-by-Bow. In doing so she ignored the dire warnings of the Matron of a Dublin Hospital where she was undertaking a pre-training course that the East End slums were a hotbed of depravity. However never one to kow-tow to authority her meeting with Grace Laing on a recruitment drive decided her fate. At a time when a home-grown supply of trainees was in short supply English hospital Matrons went to Ireland on recruitment drives. It was in Dublin's grand hotel lounges the Matrons scrutinised and interrogated prospective recruits while consuming coffee and biscuits. In Bernadette's case this ended up with a choice of hospitals in Birmingham, Liverpool, London and Manchester. It was Grace Laing; the Matron of St. Andrews Hospital in London, whose genuine interest in the prospective trainee's individual backgrounds and reasons for emigrating that decided her choice. London's East End it was.

This memoir of her SRN training is humorous, knowledgeable and a snapshot in time of a much-loved District Hospital, inspiring Matron, dedicated staff and appreciative patients. However, this is not a rose-tinted retrospective. There are no ministering angels here. Long hours and hard work put paid to that. Back street abortions, terrible injuries on the docks, chronic bronchitis, tuberculosis and life threatening childhood diseases were the reality of nursing life in an era of primitive diagnostic equipment and pharmacology in its infancy. Her description of the Juju Men is priceless as is her encounter with 'the Randy Dandy'. Other sadder tales overshadowed by the spectre of death are remembered with empathy.

For those of you looking for a stereotypical view of East End slums, misery and crime ridden neighbourhoods this is not the book for you. This East End paints a picture of a vibrant, resilient hard working people, as were the majority of East Enders. Yes, some lived in dire poverty but a spirit of camaraderie predominated, and survived being re-housed in far flung suburbs returning weekly to buy pie and mash and shop 'up the Roman'.

The author spent 25 years in Community Nursing in Tower Hamlets retiring in 2004. She still lives in Bethnal Green and remains a true East Ender.

Daughter of a Sea Locked Isle

~ Synopsis ~

This is the story of Catherine Qualter born in 1859 in the townland of Gortcloonmore, two miles down a bog road in Claregalway that was so out of the way that it was said to be 'behind God's back'. The Qualter family home was one of eleven lime washed cottages clustered together in the little Gortcloonmore colony on the Lambert Estate which were registered in 1851 in the Griffith Valuation Household Survey which was carried out to determine liability to pay the Poor rate (for the support of the poor and destitute within each Poor Law Union).

Following the Famine years want and poverty continued to be a problem and agricultural families existed as tenants-at-will, subject to the whims of James Staunton Lambert their Ascendency landlord, the will of God and the vagaries of the River Clare. In 1879, the year of 'An Gorta Beag', Catherine left home never to be seen again.

Catherine's story is told against the background of the times and the events in rural Galway that shaped her destiny.

Biography

The Author writes;

'I was born and bread and buttered in Summerhill a hard living area in Dublin. Being north of the Liffey we were 'real Dubliners'. By the mid-40's our Georgian and Regency terraces were advancing into decaying tenements but our wide streets were relatively traffic free and provided us children with an enviable freedom. They also provided hard-pressed Mammy's with hours of peace and quiet because apart from feeding any open beak that darkened the doorway the only time they saw their offspring was when they did a head count at bedtime. Even then it was not uncommon to find a cuckoo in the nest and one of your brood being scrubbed clean by a neighbour! By my 18th year I knew that I was part of a generation whose future would be on a foreign shore. Ireland, an impoverished country with a dismal economic environment and De Valera's deeply conservative theocratic government would not be able to meet either our aspirations or expectations in the furtherance of a career. Our exodus was rationalized by many families as a temporary expedient until things improved at home but I was realistic enough to know that my exile would be a long one. Early in the New Year of 1957 I 'took the boat' to start my nurse training in London's East End. Half a century later, after a long career in Public Health Nursing, and despite having Gypsy feet I have settled into retirement there' http://www.amazon.com/Bernadette-M-Redmond

Made in the USA
Charleston, SC
12 January 2017